WHEN *the* MIND CRIES...

WHEN *the* MIND CRIES...

Faith-Based Strategies to Heal Trauma,
Renew Your Mind, and Reclaim Peace

TIWALOLA OSUNFISAN, M.D.

No part of this publication may be reproduced, distributed, or transmitted in any form or by any means, including photocopying, recording, or other electronic or mechanical methods, without the prior written permission of the publisher, except in the case of brief quotations embodied in reviews and certain other non-commercial uses permitted by copyright law.

copyright@2025 Tiwalola Osunfisan, M.D

ISBN: 9798999027092

Unless otherwise noted, all scripture quotations are taken from the Holy Bible, New King James Version®. Copyright © 1982 by Thomas Nelson. Used by permission. All rights reserved.

Scripture quotations marked KJV are taken from the KING JAMES VERSION (KJV), public domain.

Scripture quotations marked MSG are taken from THE MESSAGE, copyright © 1993, 2002, 2018 by Eugene H. Peterson. Used by permission of NavPress, represented by Tyndale House Publishers. All rights reserved.

Scripture quotations marked AMP are taken from the Amplified® Bible (AMP), Copyright © 2015 by The Lockman Foundation. Used by permission.www.lockman.org

Scripture quotations marked AMPC are taken from the Amplified® Bible (AMPC),
Copyright © 1954, 1958, 1962, 1964, 1965, 1987 by The Lockman Foundation Used by permission.www.lockman.org

Scripture quotations marked TPT are from The Passion Translation®. Copyright © 2017, 2018, 2020 by Passion & Fire Ministries, Inc. Used by permission. All rights reserved. ThePassionTranslation.com

Disclaimer: The information provided by Dr. Tiwalola Osunfisan is based on her personal opinion and is for general informational purposes only. It is not intended to substitute or replace professional medical or therapeutic advice, diagnosis, or treatment. This book should not be used for diagnosing or treating health issues, illnesses or diseases. Readers should use discretion, as the content may evoke uncomfortable emotional responses. If you suspect or have a health or therapeutic concern, consult with your doctor or therapist.

Dr Osunfisan makes no representations or warranties regarding the content of this book and assumes no responsibility for any errors, inacurracies, or omissions. There are no guarantees regarding the success of applying the advice or strategies in this book, and results will vary for each individual.

By using this book, you acknowledge and accept this disclaimer.

CONTENTS

Preface   xi
Foreword   xv
Introduction   xvii

CHAPTER ONE
Psychological Pain   3

CHAPTER TWO
Hello Brain! Nice to Meet You   13

CHAPTER THREE
Common Causes of Psychological Pain   29

CHAPTER FOUR
Consequences of Emotional Pain   47

CHAPTER FIVE
Next Step in Your Healing Process   71

CHAPTER SIX
Identity Makes a Difference   79

CHAPTER SEVEN
The Pieces of the Puzzle   103

CHAPTER EIGHT
Power of Words and Biblical Meditation   121

CHAPTER NINE
The Dynamic Purpose of Prayer   141

CHAPTER TEN
The Gift of Forgiveness   161

CHAPTER ELEVEN
Attitude of Gratitude   179

CHAPTER TWELVE
Musical Delight   197

CHAPTER THIRTEEN
Nurture You   215

CHAPTER FOURTEEN
Acts of Service   239

CHAPTER FIFTEEN
Support System   255

Conclusion   277
Faith-based FAQS   281
Mental health FAQS   283
References   287
Acknowledgments   299
About the Author   301
A Note To You, The Reader: 303

To the future version of you-healed, transformed, and thriving.

PREFACE

Thank you for making **'When the Mind Cries'** a bestseller!

For a limited time, get a free digital workbook to apply the book's valuable tools and lessons at - https://transformedmindwellness.com/offerings/#book.

You'll receive your workbook and future updates from info@transformedmindwellness.com. Be sure to save the email address to prevent it from being sent to your junk folder.

A PATH TO HEALING AND TRANSFORMATION THROUGH MENTAL HEALTH AND CHRISTIAN FAITH

"When the Mind Cries" is a transformative guide that blends proven mental health principles with Christian faith to promote healing and lasting change. Whether you're seeking a supplemental tool to psychotherapy and psychotropic medication or a resource to address the limited number of mental health professionals globally. "When the Mind Cries" offers:

- *A clear understanding of the uniqueness of emotional pain.*
- *Guidance on where and how to begin your healing journey.*
- *Practical strategies to transform emotional pain into purpose.*
- *Insights into the consequences of unresolved psychological distress.*
- *Powerful tools for supporting others through their psychological struggles.*

If you or someone you know has experienced or inherited emotional pain, this book provides actionable strategies for individual and generational healing and transformation.

Dr. Tiwalola Osunfisan wrote this book to offer hope—hope that you will emerge stronger, break both personal and generational cycles of pain and bitterness, and create a better world for those around you. This book is intended to serve as a lasting guide for anyone in need of healing, including her children, her generation, and herself, whenever they feel emotionally or psychologically stuck.

FOREWORD

It fills my heart with profound gratitude to have the privilege of writing this foreword for a book that speaks directly to the deepest fibers of my being. Authored by a cherished friend and esteemed colleague, this book stands not only as a testament to her unwavering dedication but also as a guiding light through the labyrinth of mental health challenges.

Within the pages of this remarkable work lies a compilation of psychiatric insights and a rich tapestry woven from the threads of faith, compassion, and unyielding perseverance. As someone who has walked alongside Dr. Tiwa, I have witnessed her tireless commitment, boundless empathy, and unshakable belief in the healing power of connection.

Through her eloquent prose, readers are invited to embark on a profound exploration of the intricate dance between mind, body, and spirit—a journey that transcends the confines of traditional psychiatric discourse. With each turn of the page,

FOREWORD

one is enveloped in a cocoon of warmth and understanding, guided by the gentle hand of a compassionate soul who sees beyond diagnoses to the essence of human experience.

This book is more than a mere compendium of knowledge; it is a sacred offering—a testament to the transformative potential of faith, resilience, and the enduring human spirit. I fervently hope those who embark upon this journey will find solace, inspiration, and perhaps even a glimmer of illumination in the darkness.

With deepest reverence and admiration, I extend my heartfelt invitation to all who seek refuge and understanding in the realm of mental wellness. May you find guidance within these pages and the gentle embrace of a kindred spirit—a beacon of hope in a world too often shrouded in shadows.

Dr. Tola T'Sarumi
Psychiatrist,
Author of "The Mind of the Mogul"

INTRODUCTION

Hello doctor! I feel bitter about my experiences. I've done everything, yet there has been no positive change. I cry sometimes. I'm emotionally stuck.

You are NOT alone!

Regardless of sex, profession, socioeconomic status, career, race, or religion, no one is immune to psychological pain, which, amongst many things, can lead to emotional exhaustion, mental confusion, and spiritual discouragement.

The mental health crisis has revealed increased rates of common mental illnesses such as depression, anxiety, substance abuse, and suicide, with not nearly enough mental health professionals available to help.

I hear these common questions: "I'm taking my psychiatric medications and attending my therapy sessions, but the change is not as significant or lasting as I'd hoped it would

INTRODUCTION

be. What do I do next?" "I believe in God and Jesus Christ. I pray regularly. But I still struggle with emotional pain and frustration. I thought people of faith didn't have mental health challenges. What should I do?"

Let's face it. There is so much bitterness in the world! Realizing and observing this statement often leads to an overwhelming feeling triggered by diverse thoughts, including "Why is the world this wicked?" "How does one survive in this wicked world?" "Can the earth or its inhabitants be fixed?" Unresolved bitterness can lead to persistent psychological pain and frustration.

The truth is that, due to humanity's multidimensional nature, people aren't machines that can be fixed with a quick solution. They can only be enhanced by addressing their underlying needs. To effectively improve anything involving individuals—whether in organizations or families—we must have the right tools and a deep understanding of human nature.

I'm grateful to God and my parents for the blessings of being born and raised in the southwestern region of Nigeria. I'm thankful for the opportunity to have visited many countries and completed my medical education in the Caribbean, as well as received specialty and subspecialty training in the USA. This has also exposed me to the impact of culture on spirituality and mental health. As a Christian psychiatrist, transformation-led global speaker, mindset strategist, coach, and emotional and mental health ambassador, I have person-

INTRODUCTION

ally and professionally interacted with many people from diverse backgrounds.

I have observed a universal desire to be safe, loved, understood, seen, valued, and appreciated. Many of us strive for control over every aspect of our lives, which can lead to feelings of loss when unexpected events occur beyond our control. Learning to transform negativity into positive outcomes may be one of the most crucial ways to regain that sense of control.

We are thinking beings with thoughts that activate our emotions, which in turn control our actions. What goes through your mind? Do you think: "What do I do?" "How do I cope?" "How long do I persevere?" "How can I experience love again?" "I have tried it my way, but it's not working well." "How can I heal?" "Have I truly forgiven myself or others?" "How can I thrive in my marriage, career, or relationships?" "Is there hope for me while I'm incarcerated or despite the atrocious deeds I have committed?" "How can I live beyond just breathing?" "Is there a light at the end of the tunnel or a way out?" "What do I do with these negative thoughts in my head?" "Can I still praise God through it all?" "Is it time to shift from" why "to" what I should do "?"

Whether you're a teenager or an adult, curious about faith or already walking in it, and seeking to overcome psychological challenges by blending mental health with faith, this book is for you. I wrote it to help you recognize the importance of addressing your emotional pain and deepening your under-

INTRODUCTION

standing of yourself through proven mental health techniques, the knowledge of God, and the wisdom of the Scriptures. The Bible is not just any book; it is a powerful source of remedies for everything that troubles the world. You will find encouragement to confront your challenges and renew hope for a better future. This book focuses on navigating your story and supporting those around you. I will share my story alongside relevant biblical stories that you can relate to. I encourage you to have your workbook ready to get the most out of this book.

CHAPTER ONE

PSYCHOLOGICAL PAIN

The heart knows its own bitterness

— PROVERBS 14:10

Doctor, why does my heart ache? Why am I in pain? Why am I angry and sad all the time? What does psychological pain mean? Is emotional pain the same as psychological pain? Why does it feel like my mind is overwhelmed and discouraged?

I know you're hurting; I'm truly sorry.

As a physician with expertise in psychiatry and psychosomatic medicine and experience in medical and faith-based settings, I've had the privilege of supporting individuals through a wide range of challenges, both professionally and socially. I've witnessed, treated, and personally experienced the deep pain many face. Time and again, I've heard various concerns, including:

"I can't take it anymore."
"This is too painful to bear."
"Our father sexually abused my sisters and me."
"I was sexually abused by my uncle when I was a young boy."
"I was bullied in school."
"I look ugly and fat."
"I've always been told I don't sound like a lady. They say I sound like a man."
"I'm a guy who keeps hearing, 'You look like a lady!'"
"I was told by my alcoholic father that I would never become somebody in life or achieve any good thing."
"I lost my grandparents at a young age."
"I'm no good."
"I was adopted. I feel abandoned."
"Nothing is working out for me."
"I was told: 'You should have been aborted. You're a mistake!'"
"I experienced a heartbreak."
"I failed my classes and dropped out of school."
"I killed the man that killed my mother."
"I lost my wife to cancer."
"My dad was in and out of jail."
"My mom died from a drug overdose."
"I had a miscarriage."
"I was violated and abused by people in the church."
"My child was born with a health challenge."

PSYCHOLOGICAL PAIN

"I had a broken marriage."
"My young child was murdered."
"I was diagnosed with infertility."
"I witnessed domestic violence between my parents."
"I'm done trying; I feel helpless and stuck."
"I'm behind in life."
"I'm too broken."
"I feel cheated by God."
"I'm concerned about the wars that are happening in the world."
"I hate the people my parents didn't like."
"I witnessed the murder of my loved one."
"God is unfair to me."

Can you relate to any of the scenarios? Don't look around; I'm talking to you. Yes, you.

Adversity is common to humanity; no one is immune!

To address your emotional pain, you must first understand it. You can't gain control or mastery over what you don't comprehend, regardless of your background, socioeconomic status, religion, gender, age, or culture.

Unfortunately, the stigma surrounding mental health concerns still exists in many cultures, including Nigeria, where I was born, and even in the USA, where I currently reside. While it may not be as pronounced, misconceptions persist. Often, when people don't understand something, we tend to deny, criticize, or oversimplify it with phrases like,

"You're crazy or mad, go get help," or "It's all a spiritual attack." Advice such as "Suck it up," "Pray it away," or "Man up" is often offered.

These statements may be well-intended by those expressing them, suggesting that you should be resilient and not dwell on your pain. However, they often lack an understanding of the real needs of struggling people. Telling someone to suck it up without addressing their pain is like advising someone to ignore a nasty, deep wound covered with a Band-Aid instead of providing the necessary cleaning and care.

WHAT IS PAIN?

The term "pain" is commonly used to describe many things, so what exactly is pain? Pain is often described as an uncomfortable feeling that elicits discomfort and dread. Although unpleasant, pain is not bad because it signals something is wrong and requires attention.

As defined by the International Association for the Study of Pain, pain is "an unpleasant sensory and emotional experience associated with, or resembling that associated with actual or potential tissue damage." The unpleasant sensation may be from a physical or non-physical origin. It can lead to a harmful trigger and produce similar effects on the brain.

Pain results from an injury or discomfort, such as a prick, tingle, sting, burn, or ache. Pain can manifest in various ways, including sharp, dull, throbbing, or stabbing sensations. Pain is common to humankind. It's not discriminatory or selective based on race, gender, or social status.

In medicine, pain is often regarded as a symptom of an underlying medical condition. Most pain usually resolves once the unpleasant stimulus has been removed and the body has had a chance to heal. However, some pain may linger after the stimulus has been removed and healing has occurred. Pain can arise without an apparent trigger or harm.

Pain is protective; it defends the body part by causing withdrawal from the unpleasant stimulus, shielding the affected body part as it heals, and preventing the reoccurrence of such harm in the future.

Pain may be better understood as a continuum that ranges from physical to psychological due to its unpleasant characteristics.

Addressing pain is important because pain in one pillar of wellness usually affects other pillars of wellness if not adequately managed. Pillars of wellness encompass physical, emotional and mental, occupational, spiritual, social, financial, intellectual, and environmental aspects.

Pain is an integral part of animal life and vital to healthy survival. Studies show that people with congenital insensitivity to pain have a reduced life expectancy.[1] In 2001, the Joint Commission added pain as the fifth vital sign. Most things that cause disease are associated with some form of pain. Perhaps a disease develops due to a lack of comfort or peace, a *dis-ease*.

TYPES OF PAIN

Somatic or Physical Pain

Physical pain can be characterized as sharp, sudden, acute, persistent, or chronic, depending on its onset and resolution. Acute pain resolves quickly once the cause is removed. Chronic pain persists for an extended period, typically lasting more than six months. It sometimes develops if acute pain is not adequately managed. This type of pain may appear without a prior injury or persist after the initial cause has resolved. This may be due to active pain signals in the nervous system, which can continue for weeks, months, or even years.

Regardless of its origin and duration, pain may negatively affect relationships, causing feelings of rejection, abandonment, social isolation, or breakage. Thus, it can lead to social pain, affecting our thoughts, emotions, and behavior in a similar way to physical pain.

Psychological pain or Emotional pain

Psychological or emotional pain stems from unpleasant experiences that are often regarded as an unavoidable aspect of existence. Edwin Schneidman, a psychologist and a pioneer in suicidology, described this pain as "how much you hurt as a human being. It is mental suffering; mental torment."[2]

PSYCHOLOGICAL PAIN

Psychological pain is often caused by another person or a situation. This type of pain is particularly challenging due to its non-physical nature, making it difficult to explain to others as it cannot be easily touched or shown.

One of the difficulties in addressing this pain is that it cannot be accurately or reliably measured. There is no standard objective measure, such as a laboratory test like glucose levels, that most healthcare workers can interpret based on a defined range. Pain is understood and addressed according to its impact on the body. Regardless of its origin, pain can affect various physiological processes. Pain originating from a physical source seems easier to comprehend than pain stemming from a non-physical origin.

Sometimes, pain is referred to as psychosomatic if it cannot be traced to a known physiological reason or medical explanation. The term "psychosomatic" is derived from the Greek words "psykhe," meaning "mind," and "somatikos," meaning "body." Psychosomatic refers to the connection or interaction between the mind and body, indicating physical manifestations that are likely influenced by the mental state. As a physician trained in psychosomatic medicine, this happens to be my sub-specialty.

For example, persons dealing with pain often have their experience invalidated or dismissed. They are told: "Your pain symptoms are psychosomatic," or "It's all in your head," as if they are imaginary or feigned. Although statements such as these are not always made in a supportive manner, there is some truth to them. All pain is processed in our brains, as evidenced by several neuroimaging studies, which show that psychological pain affects the same brain regions as physical pain.[4] And science also shows that both physical and psychological pain tend to respond to a combination of treatments that may include medication, physical therapy, talk therapy/counseling, and lifestyle changes. In fact, certain types of medication can treat both mental health symptoms (such as anxiety and depression) and physical pain.

Frequently, we use the same words when describing physical and psychological pain, such as, "I'm hurting." "I'm in pain."

Psychosomatic medicine, now known as consultation-liaison psychiatry, has deepened our understanding of how physiological processes influence emotions and vice versa. For example, uncontrolled blood glucose levels, whether high or low, can trigger irritability, anxiety, or low mood, while chronic anxiety can lead to elevated blood pressure and heart rate. The connection between physical and psychological pain highlights the importance of addressing all aspects of health. Ignoring emotional well-being or stress when treating medical conditions can lead to complications.

Identifying the source of pain is essential for receiving appropriate care, as different types require specialized assistance from various healthcare professionals. Emotional pain must be taken seriously due to its profound impact on both physical and mental health.

Chapter 2 will explore what happens in our brain and how it affects our emotions.

CHAPTER TWO

HELLO BRAIN! NICE TO MEET YOU

For God has not given us a spirit of fear, but of power and of love and of a sound mind.

— 2 TIMOTHY 1:7

Doctor, "What happens in my brain when I'm in pain?" "Does my brain get bigger when I'm scared?" "Is my brain different when I'm depressed from when I'm not?"

Although the brain has distinct sections and functions, this book will focus on the thinking and feeling aspects of the brain. I won't bore you with medical jargon; I will delve into relevant brain structures in the following few pages. I assure you: It will be brief. This section will serve as a reference throughout the book.

HUMAN BRAIN

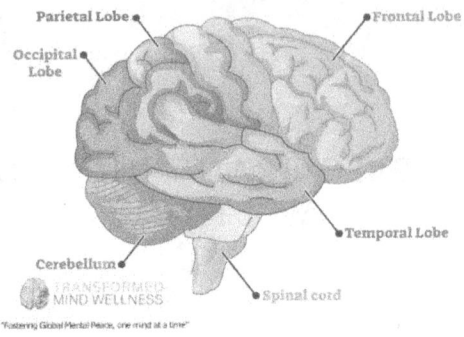

The brain can be divided into three main parts: the forebrain, midbrain, and hindbrain. It consists two halves, or hemispheres, each with distinct core regions, including the cerebrum, cerebellum, and four lobes. These lobes have specific functions, including the frontal lobe, which is responsible for executive function and personality. The temporal lobe is responsible for hearing, selective listening, and forming memory. The parietal lobe is responsible for the sense of direction and environmental awareness, while the occipital lobe is responsible for vision.

> "Men ought to know that from nothing else but the brain come joys, delights, laughter and sports, sorrows, griefs, despondency, and lamentations. And by this, in a special manner, we acquire wisdom and knowledge, and see and hear and know what are foul and what are fair, what are bad and what are good, what are sweet and what are unsavory...And by the same organ we

become mad and delirious, and fears and terrors assail us. All these things we endure from the brain when it is not healthy...in these ways, I am of the opinion that the brain exercises the greatest power in man."

— HIPPOCRATES, ON THE SACRED DISEASES
(CA. 400 B.C.)

Limbic system

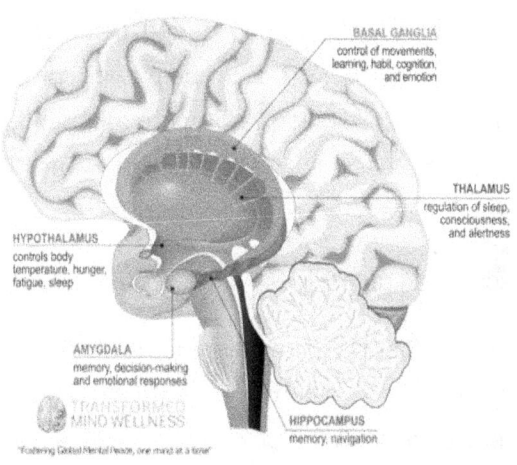

The human brain has been likened to a computer, and its operating systems can be thought of as functioning in two parts: the thinking and the feeling operating systems. The "Thinking brain" is heavily regulated by our prefrontal cortex (PFC) and its associated connections. PFC is responsible for executive functioning, which involves rational and conscious thoughts, problem-solving, comprehension, creativity, impulse control, and language.

On the other hand, the "Feeling Brain" is regulated by the limbic system, which includes the amygdala, hippocampus, hypothalamus, and their connections. The limbic system is responsible for our emotions, impulses, intuition, and instincts, which can sometimes be irrational. The prefrontal cortex and hippocampus play a crucial role in our decision-making processes.

Typically, these two systems of the human brain function in a collaborative manner. However, during stressful events, the feeling brain is more active to help with protection and survival. Relaxation techniques, such as mindfulness and deep breathing, help facilitate recovery and healing by engaging the thinking brain.

Imagine seeing a lion.

How would you feel? What would you do? What do you think would happen to your body or your brain? Panic attack? Fear? Or smiles and relaxation?

Once you see and hear the lion, your entire body perceives danger and sends signals from the environment through the thalamus to the limbic system, also known as the primitive brain. This system is responsible for emotions, survival instincts, stress levels, and memories. The amygdala, often referred to as the fear center, is a crucial component of the limbic system that processes information emotionally, particularly fear and aggression, and immediately sends it to the hypothalamus. The hippocampus collaborates with the amygdala to form and store memories from experiences.

The hypothalamus has been described as the command center or regulator of homeostasis. It establishes balance by communicating with the body through the nervous system and interacts with the limbic system to regulate the autonomic nervous system (ANS).

The ANS controls involuntary body functions such as breathing, blood pressure, and heartbeat, as well as the dilation or constriction of essential blood vessels and small airways in the lungs (the bronchioles). The ANS has two components: the sympathetic nervous system (SNS) and the parasympathetic nervous system (PNS).

The SNS activates the different stress responses. It provides the body with the energy required to fight the lion, flee from the lion (flight), or remain still and unresponsive (freeze) by sending signals to the adrenal gland to release adrenaline.

Adrenaline increases blood pressure (BP), heart rate (HR), blood glucose, and blood flow to the heart, muscles, and other vital organs. It sharpens the senses. Adrenaline also expands the small airways in the lungs, sending more oxygen to the brain, increasing alertness, and breathing rapidly.

In addition to activating the autonomic nervous system (ANS), the hypothalamus stimulates the pituitary and adrenal glands to form the hypothalamic-pituitary-adrenal axis (HPA) and releases the stress hormone cortisol. Cortisol collaborates with the autonomic nervous system (ANS) and increases energy by stimulating appetite to supply glucose from food.

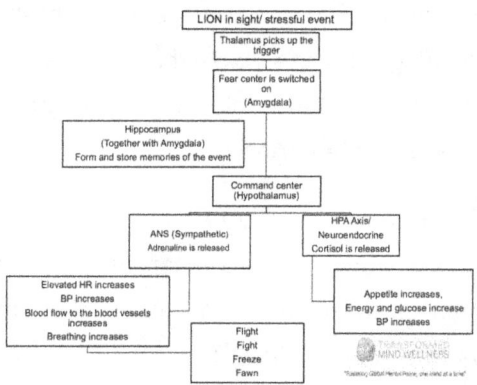

Once out of danger, your PNS takes over to ensure long-term survival.

The parasympathetic nervous system prioritizes conserving energy and is responsible for rest and digestion. The SNS and PNS are interconnected and support each other to achieve a balance. The vagus nerve, the longest cranial nerve in the body, plays a key role within the PNS.

The vagus nerve runs from the brainstem to several organs, including the neck, chest, and abdomen. It forms the bulk of the parasympathetic nervous system and relays messages between the brain, heart, and digestive system. It regulates bodily functions such as digestion, breathing, mood, taste, speech, urination, and the immune system. The vagus nerve signals to your brain that you are safe and advises you to discontinue the survival defense system. The hypothalamus activates the parasympathetic nervous system to restore physiological balance, slowing your breathing, lowering your blood pressure, and reducing your heart rate. Whew! You can relax again.

Deep breathing stimulates your vagus nerves. Vagus nerve stimulation has been tested and approved and found to be helpful with epilepsy and major depressive disorder.

In addition to diaphragmatic breathing, other vagus nerve-stimulating techniques include laughing, singing or humming, gargling, engaging in endurance activities such as jogging, cycling, or swimming, massaging the neck, shoulders, and feet, and cold-water immersion.

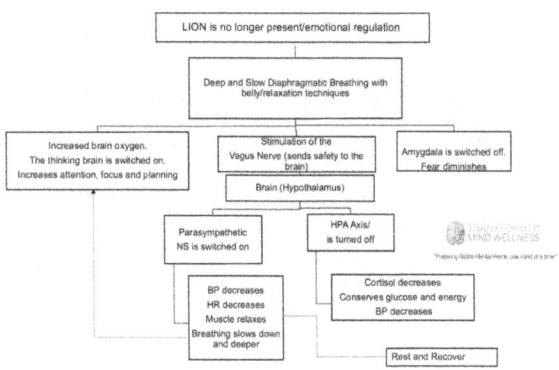

The various types of pain we encounter can be compared to the lions we face. When we feel overwhelmed, discouraged, or even frightened due to an overactive brain, it can seem impossible to move forward until we finally get a much-needed break. However, the break is sometimes not long enough before another challenge arises.

It can feel like being on a rollercoaster of different challenges. When there is persistent trauma or abuse, it can feel like constantly facing a lion. The amygdala and other brain structures remain activated, making relaxation difficult. If the **"fight"** part of the "fight/flight/freeze" response of adrenaline is not adequately managed, the response can lead to long-term physical consequences resulting in jumpiness, a tendency to startle easily, the inability to relax (the **"flight"** response), or a feeling of being immobilized or stuck (the **"freeze"** response). This is a typical response in post-traumatic stress disorder (PTSD), panic disorder, anxiety disorders, phobias, addiction, and other similar conditions. Major depression may arise from the freeze response, while people-pleasing behavior may stem from the fawn response.

The amygdala assesses people's trustworthiness, and studies have found that individuals who have suffered damage to the amygdala tend to confuse trust and betrayal. Thus, they placed trust in those who had wronged them. Our limbic system increases this effect. This region of the brain handles emotions and is also responsible for addiction.

Feelings and emotions
Feelings are processed internally and expressed externally as emotions. While there are diverse emotions in humans, including those referred to in the Bible as the works of the flesh (Galatians 5:20-21)—such as greed, envy, malice, lust, and pride—the six emotions universally experienced in all

cultures, according to Dr Paul Eckman are anger, sadness, surprise, disgust, happiness, and fear.

Acknowledging and being mindful of our feelings is essential, as they provide valuable insight into ourselves. However, it's important to remember that our feelings may not always reflect the truth. Instead, they serve as signals or clues that require further exploration. **Emotions guide us towards areas that need attention, and learning to regulate their full range is crucial. By mastering our emotions, we can utilize them to prevent self-destructive behaviors.**

It's important to recognize your feelings without becoming attached to them. Over-identifying with emotions makes it harder to move beyond them, find a resolution, and gain control. One way to create distance between your feelings and your identity is by using "I feel" instead of "I am." For example, instead of saying, "I'm anxious," say, "I feel nervous." "I am" implies permanence, while "I feel" suggests a temporary state, which helps reduce self-condemnation and allows for healthier emotional management.

Remarkably, our feelings are influenced by the memories of thoughts associated with past experiences, thanks to the library of events by the amygdala and hippocampus. **The perspective, or the meaning we give to an experience, shapes our feelings, and our feelings, in turn, shape our actions.** Therefore, being aware of the power of our feelings and emotions is critical.

Cognitive reframing, a technique that involves actively changing one's perspective on a given situation, can be highly beneficial in helping individuals regulate their emotions.

The cognitive triangle
Understanding the connection between our thoughts, feelings, and actions is crucial to our psychological well-being. Dr. Aaron Beck, an American Psychiatrist, studied this and developed a cognitive model. This is a vital component of Cognitive Behavioral Therapy (CBT), which focuses on connecting thoughts, feelings, and actions. Our thoughts are linked with our feelings. Our emotions influence our actions. Our thoughts impact our actions.

According to a 2020 study at Queen's University in Canada, the average person has approximately 6,000 thoughts daily[1]. While your mind can generate countless thoughts, it's your responsibility to decide whether to delete, keep, or reframe them.

CBT has been effective for several mental health disorders, such as depression and anxiety. This triangle is a valuable tool in our journey to identify and interrupt negative and irrational thought patterns, also known as cognitive distortions. This awareness and interruption are necessary for the change we seek to occur.

CBT is crucial in replacing these irrational thought patterns with helpful and positive ones. As Norman Vincent Peale, preacher and author, wrote, "Change your thoughts, and you change your world." This underlines the practical application of CBT and its potential benefits.

Our imagination shapes our reality, and our thoughts define who we are (Proverbs 23:7). You cannot exceed your imagination, as your actions are only as aligned with your level of thinking. No amount of physical transformation can resolve mental anguish or a negative mindset. Our mindset shapes every decision—from how we approach relationships and career choices to our leadership style and fashion preferences. It's the foundation that influences how we experience and navigate the world.

The cognitive distortions include:

- all or nothing (black or white)
- overgeneralization (focused on always or never)
- jumping to conclusions (mind reading and fortune telling)
- emotional reasoning (judging your reality based on your emotions)
- magnification (exaggerating negative qualities)
- should and must statements (focusing on overestimation and fixed ideas of expectations)
- labeling (defining yourself or someone based on an event rather than separating the person from the event)
- personalization and blame (blaming self or others for something that was due to other factors)
- mental filters (focusing on one negative fact while ignoring the good facts)
- discounting the positive (ignoring and invalidating good facts)

Examples of a negative cognitive triad

Negative thoughts: "I would never be good at anything." "I'm afraid of failing." "I have low self-esteem," etc.

Negative emotions: Persistent sadness, bitterness, anxiety, anger, etc.

Negative thoughts and emotions can lead to negative behaviors and actions, such as distractions and procrastination.

Now that you've read about the role of the brain, you may be wondering why you experience pain. Move on to the next chapter to discover some causes of psychological pain. Before you proceed, write your self-limiting thoughts, feelings, behaviors, and patterns in your workbook.

CHAPTER THREE

COMMON CAUSES OF PSYCHOLOGICAL PAIN

We know that we are of God, and the whole world lies under the sway of the wicked one

—1 JOHN 5:19 NKJV.

Doctor, "Is loss or grief normal?" "Is there a typical duration for grieving?" "Why does my neighbor believe I haven't grieved enough or that I should be over my loss by now?" "What makes me feel sad?" "What does trauma mean?" "Will I ever recover from my trauma?"

Dealing with emotional pain can be difficult because many people are not taught how to handle setbacks, challenges, or uncomfortable feelings. Rather than seeking help, individuals often try to control their emotions by avoiding pain and focusing only on positive or happy experiences.

Change is often forced upon us by the challenges we face. As humans, we desire control over things, people, and outcomes. Unfortunately, it's impossible to avoid unpleasant situations in life. **Adversity is a common experience that everyone faces. The key is in how we choose to handle it.** Winston Churchill famously said, "Attitude is a little thing that makes a big difference."

Understanding the various causes of psychological pain is crucial for comprehending why people behave and act in diverse ways. People have different experiences. This book may not cover them all, but I will try to discuss some of the most common ones under two categories: loss and oppression. Please note that this is not an attempt to downplay or trivialize anyone's pain or experiences. The goal is to identify the common features that most people with similar experiences share.

LOSS

Different types of loss can cause psychological pain. Loss can be experienced as the loss of someone, something, or an expected outcome.

Death

Losing a loved one is quite difficult because it involves a termination, often of an abrupt connection, interaction, or relationship with a loved one. This loss leads to a permanent disruption in communication between the deceased and those still living. We are left with the cherished memories of a

parent, child, spouse, sibling, relative, colleague, friend, miscarriage, pet, etc. It forces the living to accept the new truth of living without the person. Coping usually requires learning a new skill.
The death of a loved one can sometimes seem to be the most unbearable situation. The silence from the vacancy or void can become so loud, especially in the case of a child, someone younger, suicide, or a victim of murder. The death of a loved one can cause helplessness and sometimes the guilt of being alive. Survivor's guilt is wishing it were you instead of the person.

Disease
Losing health is especially difficult as we need health to do most things. Some people don't understand the worth of good health until something terrible happens. Health encompasses three key dimensions: physical, social, and mental well-being. Experiencing the declining health of someone we know or love can be challenging and emotional. It often leaves us feeling helpless and uncertain about the outcome. The more uncertain the situation, the greater the risk of emotional pain. Feeling powerless and uncertain is especially true when the person affected is a spouse, child, parent, relative, or even ourselves.
As we struggle to come to terms with the situation, the daily exposure to psychological pain can feel overwhelming. It can be challenging for people of faith who believe in God to cope with life's challenges. They may question their faith and wonder if they are being abandoned or punished for past mistakes.

Have you been impaired and limited in achieving your dreams and goals because of poor health? Suddenly, it seems hope is deferred or dashed.

Disappointment
A delay or absence of expectations can cause disappointment in oneself, a particular situation or outcome, or someone else.

Many of us may have experienced a loss of outcome. We often feel disappointed by our parents, children, siblings, coworkers, and friends, or the termination of relationships, divorce, or job losses. Disappointment can trigger a feeling of rejection as we feel less preferred or unwanted.

Sometimes, we feel disappointed in God over a delayed blessing such as marriage and childbearing. We ask questions. We may struggle with accepting that our times are in His hands (Psalm 31:15) or find it difficult to fathom how God will make things beautiful in His time. We wonder how long we will wait or if God sees or hears us. Sometimes, the most difficult one is disappointment in ourselves.

Unfortunately, the brain processes rejection and heartbreak in a similar way as physical pain,[1] activating the same areas in functional brain imaging technology.

For some, the COVID-19 pandemic ruined several plans and expectations. As multiple strains emerged, hope became deferred as everyone was forced to learn to live differently with reduced interaction and masked faces. We wondered,

COMMON CAUSES OF PSYCHOLOGICAL PAIN

"How much longer?" When will we return to normal, or is it a new normal? "How can we uncover our potential and talents to thrive?" The fear of the unknown was palpable.

OPPRESSION

Oppression occurs when an unjust display or exercise of power takes place. It's often intentionally inflicted on another person. It involves any form of abuse, bullying, discrimination, war, violence, or unfairness, either as the oppressed or the oppressor.

Adverse childhood experiences (ACEs) are events that can cause traumatic responses in children ages 18 and younger. ACEs are quite common. ACEs include sexual, emotional, and physical abuse; physical and emotional neglect; loss of a parent due to death, divorce, or abandonment; witnessing domestic violence against the mother; seeing a household member go to prison; or struggling with a significant mental health condition, or with misuse of illegal drugs/alcohol.

According to the Centers for Disease Control and Prevention (CDC), approximately 64% of U.S. adults reported experiencing at least one ACE before the age of 18 when writing this book. Nearly 1 in 6 has experienced four or more types of ACE.

Abuse:
According to the CDC, 1 in 4 girls and 1 in 20 boys aged 18 and younger experience child sexual abuse in the USA, with 91% of child sexual abuse perpetrated by someone trusted

or known by the child or child's family. 1 in 2 women and 1 in 3 men have experienced sexual violence during their lifetime.[2]

Abuse is often inflicted by those we know and trust to protect us, not take advantage of our vulnerability. I'm sorry to hear that you had a terrible experience. Please know it wasn't your fault—you didn't deserve it. Nobody should ever be taken advantage of. Perhaps you had a negative experience that wasn't sexual. Were you, for example, called ugly, worthless, or stupid? Has anyone compared you to someone else or questioned if any good can come from you? Have you experienced gaslighting? Has someone made you feel unloved, unappreciated, or devalued? Were you "traumatized" or had a traumatic response?

Trauma:
Trauma is a Greek word meaning "wound, shock, or injury." Psychological trauma is a person's overwhelming emotional response to an event. Traumatic experiences elicit complex physiological responses involving the nervous, endocrine, immune, and inflammatory systems. Trauma should not be loosely used for every temporary distressing experience that we have.
According to the American Psychological Association, "Trauma is any disturbing experience that results in significant fear, helplessness, dissociation, confusion, or other disruptive feelings intense enough to have a long-lasting negative effect on a person's attitudes, behavior, and other aspects of functioning. Traumatic events include those

COMMON CAUSES OF PSYCHOLOGICAL PAIN

caused by human behavior (e.g., rape, war, industrial accidents) as well as by nature (e.g., earthquakes) and often challenge an individual's view of the world as a just, safe, and predictable place."[3]

Sometimes, citizens of countries may experience symptoms of mental health disorders such as anxiety, depression, or post-traumatic stress disorder due to wars, racial prejudice, human trafficking, gender discrimination, kidnapping, corruption, and insecurities.

Unfortunately, we often crave or become attracted to power when we are hurt. I wish it were the power to build others, but it's commonly the power to hurt others, or, in your case, is it the power to do better? When someone wrongs you, you may be tempted to retaliate.

Have you become the bully? The abuser? Have you killed someone due to hate and bitterness? Did you make sure another lost their job because you lost yours? Are you now a player—breaking hearts because yours was broken? Do you now hate a particular race, ethnic group, citizens of a country or community, or gender? Have you allowed your pain to dictate your choices?

Have you been avoiding facing your pain? I don't blame you. **Emotional Pain can be challenging to process and accept. If we ignore our pain, life will likely make us confront it.** At that point, we must choose to deal with it or be destroyed by it. Pain can make us bitter or better; the choice is ours.

I won't claim to fully understand the context or depth of your psychological pain, as I've learned from both personal and professional experience that pain can vary significantly in severity, depth, and duration, even when triggered by similar events.

It's not your responsibility to convince others of your pain, nor should you feel the need to compare or judge the severity of someone else's suffering. **Pain is not a competition.** It's okay not to have the right or comforting words, but please avoid causing further harm by trying to provide solutions or judgments you're not equipped to offer. Sometimes, the best thing you can do is show compassion for the pain someone is enduring and encourage them to seek relief.

Trauma or psychological pain can stem from a single event or a series of harmful experiences that feel life-threatening or deeply distressing. How each person processes and responds to pain is unique. What one person considers traumatic may have a different impact on another. Rather than arguing about people's experiences, seeking to understand is often the best response. I've learned, and am still learning, not to judge what I don't understand—only God, who sees all, truly understands the depths of our pain.

We often want to control our pain immediately and desperately, on our terms. However, if not positively controlled, we recycle the emotional pain or delay the inevitable. Sometimes, we yearn for immediate justice, whether legal or spiritual; we crave validation, closure, and healing. While justice may provide some relief, it often doesn't completely resolve the trauma or restore complete healing. Still, it may emphasize the importance of seeking healing.

COMMON CAUSES OF PSYCHOLOGICAL PAIN

GRIEF

Grief is an emotional response marked by profound sorrow or anguish following a loss, particularly associated with death. Grieving is a critical process to initiate healing while gaining control over what seems to be out of our control. Ultimately, grief involves a transformation that necessitates learning to embrace our new reality.

Grief occurs in stages.

Stages of grief

I appreciate the work of Elisabeth Kübler-Ross, a Swiss-American psychiatrist who developed the Kübler-Ross model based on the theory of the five stages of grief and loss. Although these stages are explicitly based on the loss of a loved one, they could also apply to the loss of an outcome or a thing.

These stages are:
Denial, Anger, Bargaining, Depression, and Acceptance.[4]

Denial
This is the first stage. The brain attempts to manage the life-altering pain of loss. A state of shock or disbelief characterizes this stage. "No, it's not true." "How can this be happening?" As we continue to adjust to our new reality, some get stuck due to the difficulty of accepting the overwhelming pain of loss. We often wonder if we'll move on or how to do so. Denial may bring an opportunity to explore grief in bits

rather than getting crushed by a devastating flood of emotions.

Anger

This is the second stage of grief. Anger may provide an outlet for releasing overwhelming emotional discomfort. Sometimes, anger is directed at God, another loved one, the situation, or ourselves. Anger may be a preferred emotion for some, as it can be a more effective response to the fear of judgment or rejection. Unfortunately, anger may cause isolation from receiving comfort and support. If stuck in this stage, we may lose the blessings from caring communities and relationships.

Bargaining

This is the third stage of grief. It's usually characterized by helplessness and desperation. We often direct our desperation to a higher power or God. We promise to do something in return for a different outcome that minimizes or eliminates the pain. At this stage, we commonly focus on regrets and wish to gain control or change the experience.

Depression

In this phase, we are frustrated because bargaining is not productive. We begin to face the reality of our loss. We become sad as we feel the reality of losing our loved one. We become less sociable, more lonely, and isolate ourselves from others and our lives. Dealing with depression in grief can be challenging.

Acceptance

This is the last stage of grief. This phase typically involves the absence of denial, bargaining, anger, resistance, or struggle with the reality of our situation, yet we still experience sadness and pain.

Acceptance of grief aligns closely with Acceptance and Commitment Therapy (ACT), a psychotherapy that emphasizes processing unpleasant feelings without dismissing or overreacting to them. ACT helps individuals clarify their values, adding meaning to life and enhancing psychological flexibility. Developed by Steven C. Hayes, PhD, after his panic attack, ACT combines cognitive therapy and behavioral analysis. Unlike CBT, which focuses on controlling thoughts and feelings, ACT promotes mindfulness and encourages the acceptance of unwanted emotions.

While the five stages of grief are typically listed in order, please note that people grieve differently and may not experience all of these stages. Some people go through the stages in different orders. There is no specific time to grieve a loved one. Some people grieve for a few weeks, while others may grieve for several years. People also go back and forth between stages. This is all a normal process.

Grief is a personal experience. Those around the bereaved may struggle with how to provide comfort and may feel helpless. This may cause unnecessary pressure on the bereaved to hasten or halt the grieving process prematurely, causing more emotional damage.

Some people unintentionally or intentionally want to fix or provide quick relief without realizing one of the best ways to support the bereaved is by giving them space while assuring them of your availability when they are ready.

There is no perfect way to grieve. Research has revealed that attempts to deny or avoid the reality of loss can cause physical distress with a lack of ease in the body, including fatigue, weakened immune system, increased inflammation, and prolongation of other ailments.[5]

OTHER MODELS OF GRIEF

Dr. Colin Parkes, a British psychiatrist, developed a model of grief based on Bowlby's theory of attachment, which explores how emotional bonds between parents or caregivers and children influence feelings of safety, security, and connection. Dr. Parkes reported there are four phases of mourning when experiencing the loss of a loved one.[6]

- **Shock and numbness**: This is similar to Kubler-Ross's denial stage. Dr. Parkes suggests that in addition to emotional distress, there is physical distress, which can lead to physical symptoms.
- **Yearning and searching**: In this stage, we are preoccupied with the loved one we have lost. We find ways to fill the void of the loved one.
- **Despair and disorganization**: Anger may develop in this phase as we realize the loved one is not returning.
- **Reorganization and recovery**: This is like Kübler-Ross's acceptance stage. In this phase, sadness or longing is present as we move toward healing by re-

establishing some normalcy in our lives while reconnecting with others for support.

Others have suggested there are 7-stage models of grief instead of the above models.

- **Shock and denial:** We may feel emotionally numb and may deny the loss.
- **Pain and guilt:** The overwhelming pain of the loss sets in and may be accompanied by the guilt of needing more support from family and friends.
- **Anger and bargaining**: We may feel anger towards others or ourselves or pursue a bargain with a higher power in exchange for the loss.
- **Depression and loneliness**: Depression or loneliness sets in as we accept the reality of the loss.
- **The upward turn:** The intensity of the emotional pain begins to reduce as we re-establish some normalcy in our lives.
- **Reconstruction and working through:** We begin to reconstruct and adjust to our new normal moving forward.
- **Acceptance and hope:** We experience hope as we confront the reality of loss amidst emotional pain.

In the Discovery series of Daily Bread Ministries, one of the authors, Tim Gustafson, stated, "Grief is a gift." Without it, we wouldn't long for things to be made right. We wouldn't yearn for restoration to our Creator and to each other. Without grief, we wouldn't know what we're missing."

Life is a continuous process that involves navigating challenges that demand healing, surviving, and thriving. No one is exempt from this law of process, not even Jesus, even in the face of adversity. Our challenges shape and make us. Nothing great grows without pain. We can turn the pain into purpose or be paralyzed by it.

Faith doesn't make us immune to adversity; instead, faith gives a perspective and meaning that provides an advantage for a positive outcome and hope.

As a mental health professional, grieving remains challenging for me. While in college, I heard the news of several high school classmates who died from vehicle accidents and various ailments. I struggled with grief as I asked why. I am comforted by the lovely memories we shared.

I was affected differently when I lost a friend who died from breast cancer after multiple series of fasting and prayers for healing. She died from complications of chemotherapy treatment. I was shattered, especially because she had had a child shortly before. I asked God several questions about the pain in my heart.

Did God hear all the prayers?

Why did she have to die? Did she have to die from breast cancer? Was her death out of God's will? Could prayers not have preserved her from death? Were the prayers more for me and those she left behind than for her?

She was young and beautiful. Her smile was like an angel's who never took life too seriously. Her death reminds me to be kind to people. We are here today and gone tomorrow (Ecclesiastes 12.7).

Another dear friend died recently from an infection ten days postpartum. I was devastated and am still grieving her death. She was friendly, thoughtful, and had a heart of service.

I choose to take comfort in her legacy, which inspires me to be a beacon of light and support for others whenever possible. I hope this approach to the deceased's legacy is also helpful to you. In addition, writing letters to the deceased and performing acts of kindness in their honor has brought solace to my patients, clients, and myself.

While I don't fully grasp the reason my friends died, as I deepen my relationship with God, I have learned not to let what I don't understand affect what I know about God.

You, too, should stop avoiding or delaying the inevitable law of process by navigating adversity by first acknowledging your emotions and the cause of unresolved psychological pain in your life.

The next chapter will emphasize the consequences of not addressing our emotional pain, and subsequent chapters will offer tools to radically turn your emotional pain into a source of power and purpose.

CHAPTER FOUR

CONSEQUENCES OF EMOTIONAL PAIN

A healthy spirit conquers adversity, but what can you do when the spirit is crushed?

— PROVERBS 18:14 MSG

Doctor, the emotional hurt is too painful, but the thought of healing feels overwhelming. What if I can't find a way out of my psychological pain? What do I have to lose?

I understand that the emotional pain feels overwhelming, and the idea of healing can seem too much. However, remember that you don't have to do it all at once. Healing is a process, and even small steps can lead to progress. Instead of carrying the continued weight of your pain, you deserve peace and the opportunity to break free from the cycle.

Healing isn't about perfection, but about progress—and that's enough. You're worth it.

According to the World Health Organization (WHO), "Mental health is a state of mental well-being that enables people to cope with the stresses of life, realize their abilities, learn well and work well, and contribute to their community." The WHO states that mental health is "more than just the absence of mental disorders or disabilities." At the time of writing this book:

- Over 50% of people will be diagnosed with a mental illness or disorder at some point in their lifetime.
- According to the WHO, 1 in every 8 people has a mental disorder. For instance, in the countries where I'm involved, 1 in 5 Americans and 1 in 4 Nigerians (2021 WHO data) will experience a mental illness in a given year.
- 1 in 5 children, either currently or at some point, have had a seriously debilitating mental illness.
- The global prevalence of depression is 3.8% (~280 million), and anxiety varies between 0.9%–28%. They are the most common causes of disability in the world.
- The WHO revealed that data from 2000 showed that the COVID-19 pandemic has increased the prevalence of anxiety and depression by 25%.
- The CDC revealed ACEs increase the risk for long-lasting and negative effects on the well-being of a child and life opportunities such as sexually

transmitted infections, injuries, maternal and child health problems, sex trafficking, chronic diseases, education, job potential that persist into adulthood, etc.
- Data from 2022 about Parent Mental Health in America showed that parents and their teenage children report similar rates of anxiety and depression. Eighteen percent of teens reported experiencing anxiety, as did 20% of mothers and 15% of fathers. Fifteen percent of teens reported experiencing depression, as did 16% of mothers and 10% of fathers.[1]
- About 30–60% of women with PTSD have substance use disorder, and 80% of women with substance use disorder have a lifetime history of trauma.[2]

Emotional health is a key aspect of overall mental health. It's linked with physical health and other pillars of wellness. No wonder the WHO says, "There is no health without mental health." Emotional health encompasses being aware of your emotions, regulating them effectively, coping with both positive and negative feelings, and recognizing when to seek professional help.

WARNING SIGNS OF LACK OF EMOTIONAL WELL-BEING

Several people are unaware of emotional well-being, so they are unsure when it's absent.

Persistent evidence of the signs below should raise your concerns about the lack of or diminishing emotional wellness:

- Racing thoughts
- Lower energy than usual
- Lower performance at work
- Eating too much or too little
- Increased use of substances
- Sleeping too much or too little
- Easily critical of self and others
- Neglecting hygiene and personal care
- More interpersonal conflicts than usual
- Isolating yourself from friends, family, or coworkers
- Feelings of irritability, guilt, hopelessness, or worthlessness
- Reduced or lack of intimacy with God (e.g., avoiding prayer, not reading His words, etc.)

Unfortunately, people don't reach out for help because of these common reasons:

- The stigma due to cultural and societal norms
- Unforgiveness
- Pride or self-doubt
- Perfection mentality
- Comparison and competition
- Lack of identity and confusion
- Guilt from past pain and mistakes
- Limited access to behavioral health care

CONSEQUENCES OF EMOTIONAL PAIN

- Entitlement and ingratitude to God and people

CONSEQUENCES OF UNHEALED EMOTIONAL PAIN

Pain is the most common reason for doctor visits in the developed world[2], significantly impacting our functioning and quality of life[3]. It can influence decision-making, alter one's personality, and evoke feelings of shame and embarrassment, making it difficult to see opportunities for a better future.

Pain can affect how we perceive our senses, including hearing, sight, touch, and thought. It is essential to recognize that pain involves our emotions and mindset. It can make us emotionally stuck on bitter memories, making it difficult to envision a better future.

Setbacks can hinder our progress, so the Bible encourages us not to dwell on any aspect of our past to maintain a forward-looking perspective (Isaiah 43:18–19). We risk stagnation by focusing on the past instead of learning from it — whether the experiences were positive or negative.

Persistent pain can significantly limit daily activities, leading to decreased physical fitness and increased discomfort even with simple tasks. Diseases associated with pain and its comorbidities, including mental health conditions, were the leading global causes of disability in both developed and developing countries, as reported by the Global Burden of Disease study in 2013.[3]

If pain is not addressed or if it leads to prolonged suffering, it can result in feelings of hopelessness, which is a significant risk factor for suicide. Often, societal pressure, stigma, shame, and self-doubt can cause us to spend a great deal of time and energy trying to convince others of our pain. However, this same energy could be better spent exploring solutions and making progress.

Pain influences our actions—shaping what we do, why we do it, and how we make decisions about relationships, careers, and even substances like alcohol and drugs. Unresolved emotional pain can harm our sense of identity and impact the quality of our lives, experiences, and the patterns we establish, including our attractions, interests, distractions, and failures. Often, people blame others for their problems while overlooking their emotional baggage.

The hurt we carry and the dysfunction in our lives can lead us to perpetuate similar dysfunctions and negative experiences in others. Individuals who grow up in chaotic environments may be drawn to chaos, feeling uncomfortable or anxious in peaceful settings. Without healing, the repercussions can be severe and affect future generations.

Pastor Jaime Kjos, the lead pastor at Brightmoor Church, said, "Bitterness is an acid that destroys the container it's in; it takes up your past, present, and future." Choosing not to understand or heal from your pain may harden your heart and prevent you from being the God version of yourself, the best you. **Pain is a catalyst that either drives you to transformation or traps you in stagnation. How you respond**

makes all the difference. Pain squeezes out either the worst or the best in you. As Jessie Burton, an author, stated, "In suffering, we find our truest selves."

Sometimes, we may not be fully aware of our internal feelings, but increasing our emotional awareness can help us become more mindful of our mental state. Our relationships and focus often reflect our inner condition, whether we recognize it or not. Through our interactions, we can uncover our blind spots and gain a deeper understanding of ourselves.

Our decisions and choices reveal who we are, whether by chance or deliberate effort. Choices about relationships are no exception. Some relationships are seasonal, while others endure for a lifetime. You choose some friends, while others choose you based on their needs. The gift of relationships helps us understand ourselves better. Unfortunately, unresolved emotional pain can lead us to stay in an unhealthy relationship, situation, or attachment for various reasons.

To resolve the conflict around you, first resolve the conflict within you. We must address the conflict inside ourselves as we shape our environment. We become the primary environment for ourselves and others.

You may not always be able to calm the storm you're going through; however, there is a need to find peace or a resolution within yourself to navigate life so you won't lose your will to live. "The will to live sustains you when you're sick, but depression crushes courage and leaves you unable to cope" (Proverbs 18:14 TPT).

CONSEQUENCES OF UNHEALED EMOTIONAL PAIN TO SELF

"Beloved, I pray that you may prosper in all things and be in health, just as your soul prospers." (3 John 2)

We are made up of body, soul, and spirit (I Thessalonians 5:23), and pain affects us in all these dimensions. Have you ever experienced a physical headache so intense that it worsened with talking or even walking, leaving you unable to do anything but lie in bed, isolated from everyone? Eating, speaking, sleeping, and even praying become challenges.

The same is true for emotional pain; if left unaddressed, it can negatively impact your decisions, will, mind (intellect and reasoning), and emotions. Without healing, it can lead to self-sabotage and self-medication through unhealthy coping behaviors such as overeating, substance abuse, or spending sprees, further harming the body, soul, and spirit.

Emotional pain can trigger a range of physical, psychological, and spiritual issues, extending far beyond the scope of this book.

It's essential to take emotional distress seriously due to the negative impact on other pillars of wellness:

- Financial (impulsive spending or financial decisions, etc.)
- Occupational (lack of productivity at work or business, burnout, etc.)

CONSEQUENCES OF EMOTIONAL PAIN

- Intellectual (lack of creativity or wrong ideas to feel accepted, poor leadership, etc.)
- Spiritual (too tired to pray, spend time with God, attend church, etc.)
- Relational (isolation, associating with the wrong crowd, poor relationship choices, inadequate parenting, strained relationships with spouse, children, etc.)
- Environmental (wasteful energy use, pollution, etc.)
- Physical (fatigue, generalized aches- emotional distress is absorbed in the body, etc.)

Emotional pain can prevent you from setting healthy emotional boundaries with people and things. It can cause an unhealthy guard-up or the lack of a beneficial filter in your emotions, leading to poor decisions, such as people-pleasing.

Manage your emotional pain because it can make you easily controlled by people, things, and past experiences. What you don't master will oppress you, control you, and manipulate you.

If you refuse to acknowledge your pain, your body, soul (mind, emotions, and will), and spirit will malfunction, either now or later in life.

Emotional pain could cause the following:

Anger: This emotional state involves feelings of displeasure and dissatisfaction, often stemming from frustration when one feels stuck and lacks control. It's normal to feel anger toward God and believe He may be responsible for your challenges, but it's important to remember that God is a loving Father who cares deeply for you. He invites you to share your feelings with Him (Matthew 11:28-30) and desires a meaningful relationship with you.

Anxiety/Fear: Anxiety arises when persistent fears about the past, present, or future trigger the fight-or-flight response. This can lead to distrust in God and yourself, causing restlessness and irritability. Fear can isolate you from those who genuinely care and may lead to poor judgment in relationships. Fear of the unknown may also prolong periods of pain.

Fear can be defined in many ways, but my favorite is **False Evidence Appearing Real (FEAR).** It often serves as a warning to keep us safe.

When the brain perceives a threat, it activates the fight, flight, fawn, or freeze response. Techniques such as reframing, reconstructing, and deep breathing are essential for calming the brain and preventing panic.

Addiction: Addiction often stems from a desire to escape emotional pain, leading to a loss of control and potentially harmful consequences. Shame from addiction can erode social support and trigger self-criticism, making relapse more likely. Overcoming addiction typically requires rehabilitation, emotional management, and the development of healthy coping strategies. While the brain reminds us of past pleasures, self-condemnation drains the spirit and harms our relationships with God, others, and ourselves. This leads to an ongoing struggle involving the spirit, soul, and brain.

CONSEQUENCES OF EMOTIONAL PAIN

Olajumoke Adenowo, a Nigerian Architect, author, and founder of Awesome Treasures Foundation, said, "Uncleanliness and immorality are snares with the primary purpose to break a believer's fellowship with God so that they may not walk in the light and be so burdened with guilt and shame that faith becomes impossible."

Depression: This differs from occasional sadness; it is a persistent state of sadness or displeasure stemming from feelings of helplessness, hopelessness, worthlessness, or self-directed anger. It can overwhelm individuals' spirit, soul, and body, leading to isolation, neglect of self-care, and disruptions in sleep and appetite.

Distraction: *Emotional pain can divert your attention away from what you should be focusing on.* It affects focus, clarity of thought, and decision-making. Research indicates that traumatic experiences can impair concentration and memory due to decreased frontal lobe activity, shifting focus from reasoning to survival. Trauma can also trigger intrusive thoughts and nightmares, which can disrupt mental flow. Any mental struggle can interfere with attention, concentration, and memory. However, inattention does not always indicate Attention Deficit Hyperactivity Disorder (ADHD), as ADHD is often present from birth and is typically influenced by genetics or brain development.

Dissociative disorders: Unresolved trauma can lead to dissociation between the left and right brain, resulting in diminished awareness of emotions, sensations, and memories and a sense of detachment from reality or oneself. The left brain is linked to logical thinking, language, and sequential processing. When trauma causes a decrease in left-brain activity, it can lead to impaired speech production, memory loss, disorganization, and difficulties with comprehension.

Diseases: Emotional stress activates the limbic system, increasing adrenaline and cortisol levels, which can weaken the immune system and lead to diseases such as diabetes and hypertension. Traumatic responses have been linked to several diseases that "have no medical explanation." Though stress is common, prolonged and unmanaged stress can lead to negative outcomes, including insomnia, cancer, and mental health issues. Poor coping habits, like smoking and drinking, further increase these risks.

Ingratitude: Appreciating the good things from God, others, and ourselves can be difficult when we dwell on bitterness and negative experiences. Ingratitude often arises from a sense of entitlement to certain outcomes, causing us to focus on what we lack rather than our blessings. Sometimes, we forget the blessings around us, including the ability to purchase this book and the blessing of being able to breathe, read, think, and retain. I just found five things for which to be grateful. Do we have to wait until a thanksgiving occasion to be thankful? *Expressing gratitude does not require special moments; it multiplies our blessings, while disdain depletes them.*

Lost Opportunities: Our pain can cause us to overlook opportunities to bless ourselves and others. Unmanaged

CONSEQUENCES OF EMOTIONAL PAIN

emotional pain clouds our perception of support systems and growth potential.

Lack of Productivity: A positive mental environment fosters creativity, while negativity stunts it. You cannot achieve what you haven't first envisioned or imagined. Robin Sharma, a Canadian writer, stated, "Everything is created twice, first in mind and then in reality." The Bible acknowledges this in Gen 11:1–9. They built the tower of Babel in their minds before executing the project. Healing from emotional pain is essential for clarity and productivity, as a troubled heart cannot yield good results. Our heart is the soil for growth, and a desire to cultivate such a heart is life-transforming.

Prayerlessness: Unhealed pain can often cause us to project our doubts, rejections, fears, and mistrust onto God. This makes us spiritually unmotivated and weary, damaging our relationship with God. *Emotional pain should lead us to God and not away from Him.* Prayerlessness makes us more vulnerable to negative influences that inhibit spiritual growth.

Pride: Emotional pain can create a false sense of self-sufficiency, causing individuals to hesitate in seeking help. This reluctance may seem protective against future harm. However, we must recognize that we need support from God and others. Striking a balance is crucial; isolation can result in burnout. Pride can hinder genuine connections and collaboration and may ultimately be detrimental (Proverbs 16:18).

Self-Injurious Behaviors: These behaviors, such as biting or cutting, often stem from emotional numbness and a desire for relief. They may increase the risk of suicide but aren't always intended to be fatal.

Self-Criticism: Feelings of shame and guilt can lead to low self-worth (worth = value), self-esteem (esteem = respect and confidence), and self-doubt, ultimately contributing to impostor syndrome.

Suicide/Suicidal Ideation: Suicidal thoughts often stem from a sense of hopelessness that leads individuals to seek relief. While females tend to attempt suicide more frequently, males are more likely to complete the act. Although it can be difficult to predict suicide, we can assess and address its risks. Both Christians and non-Christians may struggle with these feelings, but it is important to remember that suicide is preventable.

CONSEQUENCES OF EMOTIONAL PAIN TO OTHERS

- We bleed on others. Uncontrolled pain makes us entitled to others, and we forget or lack the awareness that no one owes us anything. We may hurt others we see as enemies because they remind us of our past, and we are reactive to our unhealed pain. Unhealed emotional wounds can often cause harm to others, whether intentionally or unintentionally.

CONSEQUENCES OF EMOTIONAL PAIN

Pain can make us selfish and lead us to misbehave and disrespect others. We expect everyone else to understand why we are hurting and bleeding. **We judge others based on their actions and impact on us, but we judge ourselves based on our intentions.**

- We often criticize others harshly because we are critical of ourselves. This doesn't mean that we shouldn't give honest feedback. It's in the delivery and approach. We can provide feedback. However, it should be constructive, not destructive.
- We traumatize others. Some of us have caused traumatic experiences in others through our words and deeds during our angry outbursts, acts of violence, or agitation due to our frustration or comparison with others. Be mindful of where you release your emotions or how you express them. You may traumatize another person while dumping or venting. Be cautious about who you allow to unload their feelings on you. Be intentional!
- We hurt others. There is only so much pain the brain can endure before it leads to resentment, envy, jealousy, ingratitude, and so on. Bitterness, jealousy, and envy are common reasons why people frustrate others and create chaos rather than support one another. Some individuals take others' spouses, kidnap someone's child, commit murder, abuse, and oppress fellow human beings just to exert a sense of power and control over others.

Some people intentionally or unintentionally operate from the mindset that if they cannot be happy or have a good time, no one around them should experience any good.

- We discourage others. Emotional pain is like a door; once opened or left open, it gives access to several other harmful things. We project our fears onto others out of good intentions. Unfortunately, this may prevent them from being their best, and it can go beyond discouraging others from making productive decisions.

Church hurt

Dear church leader, member, or worker, your status or anointing level of Christianity doesn't exempt you from the consequences of unhealed emotional wounds on you and others. Committing our lives to Jesus Christ begins in the spirit and provides access to spiritual blessings. However, we need mental transformation and emotional maturity to fully experience these blessings. God is LOVE (I John 4:16) and loves people, so the damage we cause contradicts His agenda of love and reconciliation of the world to Himself. If we cannot help others, God doesn't support hurting others.

When individuals meant to be trusted in the name of the Lord cause harm, it's crucial to separate their hurtful actions from who God is. They are responsible for their behavior. Given our human nature, no one is perfect, so it is essential to manage your expectations, as they are also working out their salvation and need the grace of God. Even with good intentions, they might unintentionally spread negativity while trying to please and serve God. God should not be held responsible for our inadequacies; instead, we should be quick to rely on God every moment for strength and grace to be kind and compassionate to others (2 Corinthians 12:9). God's nature never changes. Choosing to partner with Him is a choice that requires commitment for growth. To fully utilize God's gifts and represent God to others, we must be committed to healing from our emotional pain.

CONSEQUENCES OF UNHEALED EMOTIONAL PAIN TO A NATION

A national problem can often be traced back to family and personal issues that may not have been adequately addressed. Every corrupt leader comes from a family; the same goes for a great leader. Terrorists and serial killers come from family units, and the same goes for law enforcers and joy-spreading people. If we don't heal individually, we risk hurting the country and the world.

If a country's people don't heal from a leader's harmful actions, it will affect the country's productivity, morality, safety, and health. We either contribute to territorial improvement or territorial decay.

The Bible story of the Israelites shows they struggled with what seems to have been PTSD after being in bondage for 430 years. They struggled to trust their leader, Moses, and God despite all the signs and wonders God performed through Moses. It was challenging for the Israelites to believe in the hope of a new land and victory. They intermittently indulged in immorality and self-pleasing actions, mainly because they were in bondage for so long.

When more people hold onto their emotional pain, it affects not just that generation but even subsequent generations, leading to a generational cycle of emotional pain. Regardless of your country, the same principles apply to people who make up the country. The pain of the leader and the people is the pain of the land.

INDIRECT DAMAGE/GENERATIONAL CYCLE

Since **family serves as the first classroom**, we risk creating a generational cycle of pain by exposing our children to our own painful experiences or transferring our hurt onto them. Our emotional pain is sometimes inherited and indirectly inflicted upon us. For instance, witnessing parental domestic violence or hearing about generational trauma and family conflict can contribute to negative patterns through parental modeling. Children may learn that it's acceptable to be abused or to abuse others if they observe a loved one experiencing abuse. Some children witness their parents being abused to the point of unconsciousness, being kidnapped, or even murdered. This leaves a negative impression on relationships and marriage; consequently, some children may vow never to marry. Others grow up without one or both parents, which can trigger feelings of rejection or a sense of irresponsibility. They may seek the missing piece of love through activities reminiscent of their parents. Additionally, these children might be drawn to people with similar backgrounds.

A promiscuous individual may struggle with deeper emotional pain and seek acceptance and love from the opposite sex due to feelings of rejection by a parent. Some boys might engage in legal trouble to connect with their fathers, who could be in prison or involved in illegal activities. A woman may exhibit aggression towards others, possibly influenced by her mother's treatment during childhood.

Children may face challenges in forming or maintaining relationships into adulthood because they are used to chaotic environments, which foster unhealthy codependency instead of encouraging interdependence. If parents or loved ones fail to validate the child's emotions as they grow up, potentially due to emotional neglect, this can hinder the child's ability to self-reflect and feel understood. Emotional mirroring fosters connection and self-esteem.

Children are born without significant fears or trust, without biases or discrimination, until something changes in their environments and those around them. We are shaped by what we observe, making our surroundings vital to us. We reflect on and draw from our environment.

Without emotionally stable parents or caregivers, it's unlikely that children will grow up to be emotionally healthy. **Parents must recognize their crucial role in their children's development and foster their emotional well-being. Only then can they create a stable and nurturing environment for their children's growth and wellness. An emotionally**

stable parent is essential for raising an emotionally healthy child.

Our lives are influenced by genetic (nature) and environmental (nurture) factors. Parental stress and adverse childhood experiences can predispose children to mental challenges and illnesses due to changes in gene expression without altering the gene sequences. This process is known as epigenetics.

Studies have shown that epigenetics significantly contributes to the transgenerational inheritance of mental illnesses. Thankfully, these genetic modifications are reversible, unlike the genetic changes that permanently alter DNA sequences.

Other environmental factors include a child's early experiences, upbringing, diet, exposure to pollution, social relationships, and cultural background. Providing a loving environment for children is a great gift. Love can enhance immunity and reduce vulnerability to illnesses.

It takes a deliberate effort for children who grew up in unfavorable environments to focus on seeking transformation and becoming the best possible version of themselves.

For anyone aiming to break the generational cycle, seeking healing is not just an option but a necessity.

Unhealed pain can define us, consciously or unconsciously, if we allow it. We can choose to acknowledge and redefine our pain, as Joseph in the Bible did: "I am Joseph, whom you sold…but what you meant for evil, God meant for good" (Genesis 49 and 50). Or, like me, I'm the girl who once struggled with being teased by people about the huskiness of my voice, but now I use that voice to bring glory to God and to serve humanity.

Perhaps you've identified the source of your psychological pain, and you're wondering how to heal and redefine it. I wrote this book for you.

CHAPTER FIVE

NEXT STEP IN YOUR HEALING PROCESS

Are you tired? Worn out? Burned out on religion? Come to me. Get away with me, and you'll recover your life. I'll show you how to take a real rest. Walk with me and work with me—watch how I do it. Learn the unforced rhythms of grace. I won't lay anything heavy or ill-fitting on you. Keep company with me, and you'll learn to live freely and lightly.

— MATTHEW 11:28-30 MSG

Doctor, I am committed to healing; why is faith not discussed in my holistic care? Should I discuss my faith with the therapist? Why is my church not discussing mental health? Why are my mental health providers not comfortable discussing or integrating my faith during my sessions?

I understand your perspective significantly since I grew up in Nigeria, a deeply religious country that has shaped my spiri-tual foundation, for which I am grateful. However, I have also received medical training and visited places where discussing faith may be discouraged or viewed as a broad sense of spirituality. In many cultures, spirituality, religion, and faith are intertwined with daily life, while in others, these topics are often avoided to prevent controversy.

As products of our environment, many people perceive spiri-tuality as a relationship with God or a higher power, while others view it as a personal experience of growth, connec-tion, and purpose that transcends formal religious doctrines. This distinction highlights the difference between organized religion, which involves specific doctrines and affiliations, and individual spirituality.

You believe that spirituality and faith are closely linked to emotions and mental health, while others may argue that scientific approaches should not interfere with genuine spiri-tual experiences.

Should religious rituals or psychotherapy be the sole method for emotional healing? For instance, is it enough to pray only for a person who has experienced sexual abuse? How can one separate or isolate a part of themselves without losing authenticity? Are mental health providers comfortable with faith-related discussions during therapy?

In psychiatry, spirituality is often overlooked due to concerns about bias and an emphasis on biological and psychosocial factors. The founders of psychoanalysis, who focused on evidence-based methods and quantifiable data, as well as standard diagnostic criteria, cultural attitudes, and historical skepticism, influenced this lack of discussion. This leads patients to conceal their beliefs, and clinicians to strive for professional objectivity.

However, emerging studies indicate that religious doctrines and participation can improve mental health, reduce impulsivity and hopelessness associated with suicide [1,] and serve as a protective factor against suicidal behavior. [2] This participation fosters a sense of belonging among individuals. Regular attendance at religious services is linked to a lower risk of death from various causes, including heart-related diseases and cancer, particularly in women. Those who attend more than once a week may experience a 30% reduction in mortality risk, likely due to increased social support and healthier lifestyle choices.[3]

Moreover, connecting to a larger purpose promotes resilience, enabling individuals to navigate suffering without succumbing to despair. This sense of purpose ultimately safeguards against suicidal behavior and reduces the risk of suicide. The management of emotional pain and bitterness often involves trying to resolve it on our own or ignoring it in denial or anger. Some may seek counsel from a loved one or a spiritual figure, while others may seek professional help of either psychotherapy or medication.

As a practicing psychiatrist and a Christian, I believe in the effectiveness and benefits of both psychotherapy and medication. While I wish we did not have to face the wickedness of this world in the first place, I also recognize the limitations of psychotropic drugs and the difficulties in achieving lasting improvement due to the persistent nature of psychosocial issues and mental illnesses. This frequently leads to frustration for many individuals dealing with emotional pain, causing them to seek out alternative and potentially unsafe self-help or self-management methods.

I have often been asked, "I have tried several medications and seen multiple therapists but have had only brief improvement. What else can I do?"

No human being has the power to cure or fix another human being's mental and emotional struggles without the help of the Creator and Maker of human beings. Our professional abilities focus on equipping you with a tool kit for coping with that difficulty, which may include psychotropic medications or therapy. Healing is primarily an internal process before it becomes external. Healing is possible thanks to neuroplasticity, a phenomenon that occurs throughout childhood and adulthood as new pathways and connections form in the brain.

Through my observations and interactions with various individuals, I have found that while the therapeutic modalities mentioned earlier can be beneficial, maintaining a consistent connection with God, mainly living purposefully with an awareness of His love, is often essential for sustaining those benefits throughout the healing process. I have noticed that individuals who explore their Christian faith alongside mental health support—such as psychotropic medications and therapeutic modalities—often find renewed hope and meaning in their suffering.

Although incorporating spirituality into psychological practices, such as spiritually integrated CBT, has been shown to reveal meaningful paths out of despair and help reduce suicide rates, [4] not every mental health provider or faith-based leader is comfortable with this approach due to limited education, religious biases, diverse preferences, and experiences. While spiritual themes may not fit neatly into diagnostic manuals, I believe they are essential for addressing the holistic needs of patients, requiring a genuine multidimensional understanding and a judgment-free approach.

In the upcoming chapters, you'll explore faith-integrated tools for managing emotional pain and regulating your emotions. But before you dive in, I would like to introduce **ADAPT-faith™**, a framework that has helped me navigate challenges in my own life. While its principles are simple, they've equipped many clients and loved ones who've embraced them. This actionable and practical approach will serve as a backbone for the upcoming strategies, integrating Godly beliefs and therapeutic strategies when facing emotional struggles.

As you work through the chapters and the accompanying workbook, you will be prepared to embrace change and transformation. The workbook will guide you in applying these principles, enabling you to take action in real time.

Here's a breakdown of the ADAPT-FAITH™* framework:

- A: Acknowledge your emotions and thoughts.
- D: Discover God's presence through His word, prayer, and past faithfulness.
- A: Ask for the lessons you can learn and adopt a mindset shift.
- P: Prioritize what you can control and trust God with what you can't.
- T: Take responsibility for your actions and reactions.

I hope this framework becomes a valuable part of your healing toolkit, guiding you as you navigate emotional pain and make lasting changes. Remember, you may need to learn, unlearn, and relearn to adjust, but whatever the case, embrace change as your friend.

---

* **ADAPT-FAITH™** is not yet a validated tool, and Transformed Mind Wellness, LLC does not assume liability for its application. If you're interested in validating **ADAPT-FAITH™** or sharing a testimony, please reach out through www.transformedmindwellness.com/inquiries

CHAPTER SIX

IDENTITY MAKES A DIFFERENCE

But you are a chosen generation, a royal priesthood, a holy nation, His own special people, that you may proclaim the praises of Him who called you out of darkness into His marvelous light.

—I PETER 2:9

"Doctor, I'm confused about who I am. I struggle with my self-worth, and people's opinions bother me; what do I do?" "I don't like myself. I'm quick to please others; I believe I'm worthless and a failure. How can I change this?" "How can I stay true to myself?"

Your identity is the cornerstone of your existence. It's the answer to one of life's most important questions. Knowing who you are, what you stand for, and what you want to achieve is essential. Your identity shapes your decisions and ultimately determines your destiny. Discovering yourself can guide you toward a fulfilling and purposeful life.

Self-discovery leads to self-development, which in turn leads to self-mastery and ultimately to self-actualization. Dr. Myles Munroe, a Bahamian evangelist, stated, "The greatest discovery in life is self-discovery." Until you find yourself, you will always be someone else. Become yourself."

Identity shapes our perception of experiences. Our perspectives shape the meaning we attribute to what happens to us, which in turn influences our thoughts, feelings, and actions. Identity can either delay or accelerate the process of self-development and self-actualization.

Frequently, people define themselves based on their experiences. Your challenges or psychological pain do not define you. Should you call yourself a failure because you failed at something? Should you ignore the difference between a failure as an event and a failure as a person? Eckhart Tolle, a German writer, said, "As long as you make an identity for yourself out of pain, you cannot be free of it."

OUR EXPERIENCES

The truth about our experiences is that they don't have to define us. However, they influence, shape, and help us understand our identity. Identity is multifaceted and involves our experiences, values, beliefs, and relationships, which help create a continuum of our self-image. It's formed by

IDENTITY MAKES A DIFFERENCE

unique physical, mental, emotional, social, spiritual, and interpersonal characteristics.

A dollar bill remains a dollar bill, even when it's torn. When put back together, it still holds value for making a purchase. Water is water, regardless of its form; however, it exists in various states depending on the environment. Ice doesn't change the fact that it's water; it simply has a different state. Water in a bowl or on the floor is still water. It remains water in the morning, afternoon, and evening. Seasons may influence its appearance, but they do not change its essence as water.

A prince is from a royal family. Regardless of his experiences, he remains a prince. His experiences would lead to a deeper understanding of himself, including his values, beliefs, eating habits, style of dress, and manner of speaking. His experiences would also enable him to discover, develop, and deploy his uniqueness, talents, gifts, and purpose. The lack of self-awareness or understanding of his identity as the royal heir to the throne limits his ability to function effectively in royal roles.

Even when babies trip or break things, they still have their identities. These experiences don't alter the fact that they are babies and certainly don't change the potential for them to grow into adults; instead, these experiences contribute to their development.

The metamorphosis of insects such as butterflies occurs in stages: egg, larva, pupa, and adult. Although each stage has a different phase of transformation that involves differences in timing, shape, form, and growth requirements, none of the stages can be skipped, as each stage must occur to contribute to the end result of an adult butterfly. Some experiences occur due to our unique identity or life purpose. These experiences are processes that must happen in all dimensions of life to equip us with the tools necessary for our life journey and purpose.

Although our experiences can change, certain core aspects of our identity remain constant. Also, in our lives, we may be abused, persecuted, perplexed, crushed, violated, oppressed, and taken advantage of. None of these changes our worth (2 Corinthians 4:8–10). Worth is not determined by human experience but by the Creator of our lives (Isaiah 43:4).

Growing up, I struggled with embracing my voice. It was deep and husky, and I couldn't help but wonder why. People would tease me, saying I sounded like a boy with a baritone voice. Some of them meant it as a compliment, but I found it hard to accept. I felt my voice set me apart from my siblings, and I just wanted to fit in. I didn't understand why I felt that way, and I didn't have anyone to confide in at the time. It seemed like everyone around me was perfect, and I felt so alone in my struggle.

As a result, I began wishing I were a boy. I dressed like a "tomboy," sometimes wearing my brother's clothes and shoes. It made me feel more comfortable and matched the comments about my voice.

I embarked on a journey filled with pain and uncertainty, but it ultimately led me closer to God. The more I sought Him, the more I discovered His deep love and thoughtfulness toward me. As I delved into the Bible, I stumbled upon scriptures that resonated with me, emphasizing His unconditional love and deliberate creation of me.

Psalms 138:14 and Jeremiah 1:5 particularly resonated with me. They made me realize that the creator of the universe not only knew my name but also intentionally fashioned me. I uncovered my uniqueness and the truth that I was fearfully and wonderfully made. I was not a mistake; I was intentionally created as I am with a purpose.

Through prayer, fasting, and meditating on the scriptures, I was constantly reminded of His love for me, and I found solace in the fact that I was never alone. I felt known, accepted, seen, and loved for exactly who I was. I no longer felt the need to pretend or blend in; instead, I embraced the fact that God had designed me to stand out uniquely for His pleasure.

My experiences made me realize that having the right mindset is vital to conquering any challenge. Our experiences should not define us; they should aid our growth and shape our identity. It became clear that one can be gifted yet still wounded. While the anointing or gifts may bring challenges, they also foster growth.

With my knowledge of God, I stopped longing for someone else's voice or wishing I had been made differently because I realized that God doesn't make mistakes.

As a result, I refused to hold anyone responsible for the past or any future teasing I may encounter. I chose to view my struggles with my voice not as discouraging but as a blessing that led to personal growth and self-discovery. It provided me with opportunities to assist others, including my patients and clients, in overcoming obstacles and living authentically.

Though I still encounter remarks about my deep voice and am occasionally mistaken for a male over the phone, I have decided not to be upset or frustrated. Instead, I kindly correct them and move forward.

I strive to live intentionally, guided by values aligned with my purpose: to bring glory to God and inspire transformation in others. Alan C. Fox, author and founder of Rattle Poetry Journal, once said, "Your actions are the true statements of your identity."

Indeed, I continue to face struggles and make mistakes, but I no longer allow them to define me. I recognize that they are meant to equip, empower, and aid me on my life's journey.

We can't recover or deal with pain without first understanding our identity from a holistic perspective. It's essential to know who you are and, more importantly, to know *whose* you are; this knowledge will help you with your identity. The discovery of our creator reveals who we are. Without awareness of our identity, there is confusion. **You cannot understand the why of your experiences without understanding who and whose you are.**

IDENTITY MAKES A DIFFERENCE

Who are you?

Identity is the set of characteristics that sets an individual apart from others.

What distinguishes you? What makes you unique? Even identical twins may share some bodily features and other similarities, yet they still possess distinct fingerprints, iris scans, personalities, preferences, values, and core beliefs. In the following pages, I will share psychological theories that help us better understand our identity.

Identity, according to the American Psychological Association, is defined as:

> *An individual's sense of self is defined by (a) a set of physical, psychological, and interpersonal characteristics that is not wholly shared with any other person and (b) a range of affiliations (e.g., ethnicity) and social roles. Identity involves a sense of continuity or the feeling that one is the same person today that one was yesterday or last year (despite physical or other changes). Such a sense is derived from one's bodily sensations, one's body image, and the feeling that one's memories, goals, values, expectations, and beliefs belong to the self. Also called personal identity.* [3]

Identity was the primary focus of Eric Erikson, a German-American developmental psychologist and psychoanalyst known for his theory of human psychological development. According to Erikson's autobiographical notes, as cited by

Daedalus, he coined the phrase "identity crisis," which refers to a conflict related to any of the eight stages of psychological development.

The eight stages are:

- Infancy – Basic trust versus mistrust
- Toddler – Autonomy versus shame and doubt
- Preschool-age – Initiative versus guilt
- School-age – Industry versus inferiority
- Adolescence – Identity versus identity confusion
- Young adulthood – Intimacy versus isolation
- Middle age – Generativity versus stagnation
- Older adulthood – Integrity versus despair

Identity versus role confusion is the fifth stage of the eight stages of psychological development. This stage involves asking, "Who am I?" and typically occurs during adolescence, between the ages of 11 and 18, as individuals explore the independence of social relationships to develop a strong sense of self.

Erikson believed that not completing this stage leads to role confusion, as one lacks understanding or is disappointed in oneself. Engaging in out-of-control behaviors may reflect an identity crisis. **Several factors, including hormonal differences, genetic makeup, family members, friends, schoolmates, societal norms, role models, and trends, all contribute to the development of an identity.**

The fifth stage is critical to a child's development, as it's responsible for forming ambitions, setting college goals, learning, and establishing boundaries, all of which contribute to gaining independence in life decisions, including obtaining a driver's license and choosing a college. Unfortunately, this is also the stage of significant peer pressure to conform to the cultural, hormonal (puberty with bodily changes), and social expectations with fear of missing out (FOMO).

Many critical changes happen during the fifth stage. If not handled properly, lifelong consequences and intergenerational pain may result. Several adolescents of this age struggle with confusion. If little to no self-awareness and intentional positive changes are achieved, the confusion may persist into old age.

Personality

We cannot discuss identity without understanding the various components of our personality. Your personality is a broad term for a unique set of behaviors, traits, and emotions that typically determine your behavior.

According to the American Psychological Association:

> *"Personality refers to the enduring characteristics and behavior that comprise a person's unique adjustment to life, including major traits, interests, drives, values, self-concept, abilities, and emotional patterns. Various theories explain the structure and development of*

personality in different ways, but all agree that personality helps determine behavior."[4]

Personality elements
Sigmund Freud, an Austrian neurologist and founder of psychoanalysis, proposed that personality consists of three components: the id, the ego, and the super-ego, which collectively shape human behavior.

The id is the unconscious part at birth, driven by instinctual desires that seek the immediate gratification of bodily needs, such as hunger and aggression. It operates without reasoning, leading to impulsive behavior.

The ego serves as the realistic mediator between the id and the superego. It organizes thoughts and employs defense mechanisms to balance the id and super-ego. Ego development reflects cognitive function and self-awareness.

The super-ego develops around age five and represents morality shaped by parental beliefs and societal norms. It seeks to delay gratification and works to balance these conflicting desires.

Personality traits:
You may be familiar with the universal Big Five personality traits, which were developed in the 1980s. They are:

Openness to Experience: Characterized by appreciation for art, emotion, adventure, and curiosity. Open individuals are more creative and willing to engage in new experiences.

Conscientiousness Is Characterized by self-discipline, organization, and a drive for achievement. High conscientiousness may be seen as stubborn, while low conscientiousness reflects spontaneity but may seem unreliable.

Extroversion: Characterized by energy from social engagement. Extroverts are enthusiastic and enjoy interacting with others, whereas introverts tend to prefer solitude and form deeper, more meaningful connections.

Agreeableness: Characterized by the desire for social harmony, kindness, and trust. Agreeable people are cooperative and considerate, while disagreeable individuals can be competitive and skeptical.

Neuroticism: Characterized by emotional stability, with neurotic individuals experiencing strong negative emotions and heightened stress.

Human personality is complex and can be understood through various frameworks. While behavior and personality are distinct concepts, they are interconnected.

Behavior refers to the observable actions of an individual in response to different situations. In contrast, personality encompasses the unique traits, characteristics, thought patterns, emotions, and behaviors that define a person's identity. While behaviors can change more easily, personality traits tend to be more stable over time. Temperaments such as phlegmatic, choleric, sanguine, or melancholic represent inherited patterns [5] of behavior that influence energy levels and emotional responses. Although personality traits may evolve as we age and encounter new life experiences, our temperaments tend to remain relatively consistent.[6]

Several personality assessments, including the Myers-Briggs Type Indicator (MBTI) and DISC, reflect how genetics, environment, preferences, experiences, and role models shape our thoughts, emotions, and behaviors. Most people have a mix of these traits, reflecting the complexity of human nature.

We are multi-dimensional and should deepen our understanding of ourselves and our relationships. *If you seek emotional intelligence and mastery, self-awareness is a valuable gift you can give yourself*. While these assessments do not reveal everything, they can help you explore different aspects of your identity, highlighting your strengths, limitations, and opportunities for growth. Enhancing self-awareness can improve communication, relationships, leadership skills, and various facets of your life.

The role of science
Our bodies are made of deoxyribonucleic acid (DNA), which contains the genetic code in every cell. It consists of four-letter codes: Adenine (A), Cytosine (C), Thymine (T), and Guanine (G), which are under intelligent instructions to create us. The genetic material is divided into 46 separate chromo-

somes. Each cell contains two copies of this genetic material, comprising 6,496,660,000 bases per cell.[1]

The human genome comprises approximately 3.2 billion individual bases. Based on the measurement of cell density in each tissue type, it's estimated that an average adult body contains approximately 37.2 trillion cells.[1] The exact number can vary based on age, body size, and sex.

Each cell contains approximately 2.14 meters of DNA, resulting in a total DNA length of 79,608,000,000,000 meters, or 79,608,000,000 kilometers. The moon is only 384,400 km away, and the sun is 150,000,000 km away. This means that the DNA in your body could stretch from the sun to the Earth 530 times, although it would still weigh only 2.6 kg.[1]. The DNA will stretch around the entire solar system twice.

Each DNA molecule comprising our genes accumulates chemical marks that influence how much a gene is expressed. The epigenome is the collection of chemical marks. Different childhood experiences rearrange these chemical marks. This is why genetically identical twins can have different behaviors and skills. The epigenome can determine whether or how genes express or release the information within them.[2]

Some people focus so much on science only, which can confuse some Christians. The ideology that faith and medicine (in this case, mental health) are mutually exclusive has caused more harm than good, especially for those who identify solely with medical science or faith.

Science is not the opposite of God but an extension of God. Science is the aspect of God that has demonstrable evidence within the human realm.

Your spiritual identity

Knowing your core identity in God is essential, regardless of how you came to be on Earth, your hormonal differences, upbringing, genetic makeup, or the spectrum of personality traits. As mentioned in Chapter 4, we are spiritual beings with a soul residing in a body to function on Earth, a tripartite nature preserved by God (1 Thessalonians 5:23). Our soul has emotions (Isaiah 61:10), a will (Job 7:15 and Job 6:7), and a mind to think and reason (Proverbs 2:10).

During creation, God made heaven and the earth, the inhabitants (Genesis 1:1–2), and He called everything He made good (Genesis 1:31). God created humankind in the image of the Trinity with a spirit and a soul and gave us dominion over the earth. Yes! God is Spirit and has a soul (Leviticus 26:11). He gave us a body made from dust to function on earth because for any spirit to function fully in a particular region, that spirit requires partnership with the inhabitants or must attain the form of that region (Genesis 1:26 AMP).

The universe didn't create us! If you're observant, you will notice that it must have required more than a mistake, a coincidence, or a bang to form the world and its inhabitants. There must have been a purposeful intelligence and a master plan to account for approximately eight billion people from diverse ethnicities, nations, and languages.

IDENTITY MAKES A DIFFERENCE

How can you fully understand why you were created or why you exist? You discover the creator's intention by asking, "What did you have in mind?" Why did you make me?

While many factors contribute to our identities, the impression of the Creator is the most crucial. You cannot be who God intended you to be without being aligned with His ways.

If you take a fish out of the water, it dies. If you remove trees from the soil, they die. When a man disconnects from God, he dies in spirit and soul (Acts 17:28). God is our source and dwelling place. We were made to live in His presence and will.

Sometimes, we forget who we are. If a prince forgets he is born into royalty, he will not discharge his duties as a prince. He will be unaware of his authority, resources, and opportunities, including all that belongs to the king, which will prevent him from fulfilling his potential as an heir to the throne.

This was the experience of the prodigal son and his brother in the Bible. The prodigal son lost everything before he realized that his true inheritance was his sonship, not his material possessions (Luke 15:11–32).

God, the King of kings, is great in every way. We must function like God on earth if we have His spiritual DNA. When we are confused about our spiritual identity, we are robbed of our inheritance, resources, and opportunities (Galatians 4:1).

The Israelites struggled with their new identity as God's chosen people in the Old Testament. Despite God's blessings and wonderful works, they wrestled with past emotional pain, which in turn led them to doubt God's promises and hindered their healing.

Perhaps they experienced symptoms of PTSD, resulting in confusion about their identity. Their doubt in the supremacy of God, despite His faithfulness and miraculous signs, caused them to miss or delay the blessing. This may resonate with your experience, even though you are chosen by God (I Peter 2:9).

Identity is fundamental, particularly in relation to past or current traumatic experiences.

The term "Christian" was originally used by non-believers to describe the followers of Jesus rather than by the believers themselves or by Jesus (Acts 11:26). Christianity should not be limited to religious practices and rituals; instead, it should focus on our commitment to Jesus' teachings regarding our identity in God and our relationships with God, others, and ourselves. This underscores the importance of understanding who you are by deepening your awareness of whose you are —recognizing your connection with God and humanity. True Christianity should be a consistent and authentic way of life rather than merely a seasonal garment.

IDENTITY AND INTEGRITY

Confusion or a lack of awareness and clarity about our identity can lead to a lack of integrity, which in turn affects our perception of God and our relationships with others.

Integrity is defined as being undivided, whole, consistent, complete, sound, and incorruptible. The opposite of integrity is hypocrisy, and hypocrisy is widespread. Practitioners of hypocrisy vary depending on the setting, situation, and people involved. They pretend to have or maintain a particular reputation. This is why people sometimes struggle to make decisions about others. They are inconsistent in their values, words, and deeds. They contribute to the reason some people struggle to trust others.

Integrity is who we are everywhere and every time. Integrity involves authenticity. Rick Warren, an American author and preacher, said, "Integrity means you're the same person with everybody, in your speech, actions, and motives, no matter which part of life you're dealing with."

To be 100% consistent, we need the superior grace and power of God, the all-powerful One.

Spending time receiving God's power to be trustworthy and reliable to ourselves and others is essential. Understanding human nature helps us manage our expectations of others more effectively. Many of us struggle to keep our words to ourselves or others. We lie and do things to please others while displeasing ourselves and God. Our desire to control people's perception of us can lead to people-pleasing, which is exhausting and costly. We should recognize our limitations and capacity when challenging ourselves to achieve goals.

I have learned it's so important to know who said the words. Does the person have integrity? If God said it, don't respond to your situation based on your feelings or emotions but on the knowledge of God.

I have realized that when we say we are the children of God, people don't care about how perfect we claim to be. They are more concerned about how God's amazing grace has changed them and how it can change others. Not everybody wants to know how you've never sinned; instead, they are more interested in how you overcame the struggle, found strength in your pain, and how your challenges contributed to your growth because it gives them hope. People are looking for the light in the darkness.

Jesus didn't come for the perfect, the righteous, or the qualified, but He can qualify the unqualified by His righteousness. "I have not come to call *the* righteous, but sinners, to repentance" (Luke 5:32 NKJV).

ACCEPT ALL SHADES OF YOU.

Without your consent, no one can make you feel like a second-class citizen or less of a human being. Whenever you're in doubt, remind yourself or the person (including the devil) of your value and worth, which are sustained and guaranteed by the unconditional love of God and the blood of Jesus.

We are not defined by education, age, financial status, emotions, political views, body image, Facebook/Instagram likes, or how we feel about ourselves on any given day.

IDENTITY MAKES A DIFFERENCE

Instead, we are who God says we are. The earlier we acknowledge, accept, and believe the truth, the better it is for us: We are loved unconditionally, not by our works, but by God, who loves the imperfect, the broken, the messed up, and the weak (Psalms 147:3).

Be original and authentic. The best you can be is the best version of you, not someone else. Oscar Wilde, an Irish poet and playwright, stated, "Be yourself; everyone else is already taken." You can be inspired and motivated by people's successes and stories, but wanting to drop everything about you to become exactly like others is a sign of deeper problems.

Through my life experiences, and especially with my voice, I have learned to be authentic by knowing *whose* I am, who I am, what I have, and why I'm here. I'm aware of the different seasons of my life and where I'm headed after this one.

Understanding your uniqueness should foster authenticity, not inferiority. Regardless of how you came to this world, you're not a mistake but His workmanship for good works (Ephesians 2:10). Your mistakes don't define you. God's love accepts you the way you are.

God's love doesn't leave us the same but transforms us into the image of Jesus daily. He gave all to us. God improves whatever we give Him. His love adopts us through confession and faith in Jesus.

The good, bad, and ugly have contributed to who you are today or will become. A single aspect of your life doesn't produce the total value of your life, just as you cannot choose only one side of the coin to pay for a transaction because neither the head nor the tail of a coin provides the complete value of the payment. You may struggle with low self-worth, low self-esteem, and self-rejection if you refuse to acknowledge a side of yourself, no matter how terrible it is.

Self-acceptance doesn't negate the need for self-improvement; they can coexist. Accepting yourself doesn't mean being content with your negative traits. Instead, it means recognizing your human imperfections, acknowledging your positive qualities, and committing to personal growth with humility.

God likes variety and uniqueness; He intentionally made you different. The time zones are different, and the seasons are distinct. God delights in the diversity of thoughts and ideas, which brings glory to His name. Look at your body; there are many parts. Imagine if you only had a head and didn't have feet (1 Corinthians 12:12–31).

Embracing your multi-dimensional identity can lead to greater contentment and help you avoid unproductive comparisons. You already possess what you need for your unique life journey and purpose. It's essential to focus on your path and make the most of your life. Debola Deji Kurunmi, a Nigerian coach and preacher, stated, "Walking in someone else's purpose without grace will lead to disgrace."

Grace is available to all through Jesus; sonship is not something that is earned. Stop trying to earn God's love; you can't! It is unconditional. Start resting in it. You are

loved! No *ifs*, *ands,* or *buts*. So, you do things not for His love but from His love. Living every moment from the consciousness of His love and the clarity of your identity will influence your decisions.

Do you struggle with feelings of not belonging, low self-worth, or feeling unloved? Some struggle with self-worth or unworthiness or may think it's the same as confidence. Rejection doesn't indicate a lack of worth. Instead, it's when you or someone else fails to recognize and appreciate your value and potential. Remember, your creator determines your value, not someone else's opinion.

Confidence is your belief in your abilities and capabilities, built on self-worth. Self-esteem is how you value yourself. Your identity shapes self-worth. A lack of self-worth influences how we present ourselves to others and how we live our purpose.

Your self-worth doesn't fluctuate; it's consistent. While there are rewards and recognitions earned based on your service and contributions to others and the world, your self-worth is not tied to external experiences, such as successes, level of education, socioeconomic status, job, number of friends, marriage, position, social media following, or earthly possessions.

God loves us unconditionally and has given us the right to belong through the sacrifice of His Son, Jesus (John 1:12–13).

Perhaps identity is not a struggle for you, or it's not the only one you face. Maybe you now have a better understanding of who you are, but you want to know why you had to go through your psychological challenges. The next chapter may be what you need to acknowledge: everything happens for a reason.

CHAPTER SEVEN

THE PIECES OF THE PUZZLE

To everything, there is a season, A time for every purpose under heaven.

— ECCLESIASTES 3:1

"Doctor, I'm aware of who I am, but I don't know why I'm struggling psychologically." "Why was I abused?" "Why did my child have to die?" "Why do I have a terminal disease?" "Why did I have to experience the loss?" "The disappointment?" "Why me?" "Is God aware of what happened to me?" "Did He really see what happened to me?"

I'm sorry to hear that you've faced those negative situations. I understand that these experiences can lead you to question the validity of your faith or feel like giving up, especially when life's challenges seem unending and overwhelming.

Life's difficulties can bring even the strongest individuals to their knees, as no one is immune to adversity.

It's essential to recognize the multidimensional aspect of our identity, particularly our tripartite nature, as we navigate life's challenges. However, even with this understanding, maintaining faith is not always easy—especially when we don't comprehend what is happening around us or the big picture. True faith requires us to trust in God's nature, even when times are tough and the path forward is unclear.

I wish I knew the exact reason you went through or are going through this painful situation. I know you may struggle with the thought of how something that caused pain can have some good in it. Can anything good come out of something traumatic or heartbreaking?

I know that not knowing the reason can be frustrating and may lead you to ask, ' Did I have to lose something or someone to gain an improvement or receive another blessing?' You may have tried many medications and strategies to be able to handle the emotional pain, but it seems you cannot get over the lingering question of why.

Sometimes, the healing process of emotional pain is tolerable when we understand its purpose.

No one asks for emotional pain, which usually comes without permission, sometimes with an initial setback and slowed pace, or so it seems to us until we choose how we want to use the emotional pain.

An issue is usually not limited to the event that caused it; our response also influences it. Our capacity to adapt and cope with challenges is a vital component of our emotional intelligence and resilience.

As infections strengthen our immunity, challenges help build our mental strength.

All events can bring about change and grief, which involves letting go of the past and accepting the new reality.

If you choose to remain stuck, you limit yourself and hinder your growth. Instead of feeling trapped, try shifting your focus from what you can't control to what you can. Rather than dwelling on the discomfort of your situation, consider not only why this is happening to you but also how you can turn it to your advantage by finding meaning in it. Adopting a different perspective can lead to success. The mindset that makes you feel stuck may not be the same one that will help you move forward.

The meaning we attach to an experience determines the kind of life or outcome we will have. If we choose to focus on the positive lessons from an incident, we will have more positivity; conversely, if we choose to dwell on negativity, we will have more negativity.

This was important to Dr. Viktor Frankl, a Jewish-Austrian psychiatrist who developed logotherapy before his deportation to a concentration camp in Germany.

This therapy is based on an individual's primary motivation: finding meaning in life. Dr. Frankl's work emphasized the significance of finding meaning in life's events. He suggested that work and suffering can lead to this meaning, ultimately resulting in fulfillment and happiness.

We cannot perform at our best capacity if we don't understand the reasons behind our unhealed emotional pain, especially when it feels like a detour from our original plan or expected outcome. To grasp the purpose of our experiences, we must first comprehend the deeper significance of our existence. This is especially true because when the purpose of something, including our experiences, is not understood, it is likely to result in a malfunction, misuse, or breakdown. Dr. Myles Munroe said it beautifully: "When the purpose of a thing is not known, abuse is inevitable.

Each experience is a vital piece of the puzzle that forms the bigger picture. Criticizing one piece or a section of the puzzle for not being complete would be premature and misplaced, just as it would be for you or others to criticize who you are while you are still in the process of becoming. Like this book, each chapter conveys a message that contributes to the overall theme, and we cannot fully understand the book until we reach its conclusion. You may feel your painful experiences have no end, but remember that these challenges are merely temporary chapters in your story, not the final chapter. They are all part of the journey leading to a brighter future.

THE LAW OF PROCESS

Everything in life has a purpose and operates in seasons (Ecclesiastes 3:1-2), with preparation for each season being

THE PIECES OF THE PUZZLE

an essential part of the process. This can be challenging, especially when it feels prolonged, but it's often necessary for our growth and equipping.

Just as we can't plant a seed today and expect a harvest tomorrow, we must embrace the process that occurs between planting and harvesting, no matter how complex it may be. Mark 4:28 (KJV) reminds us: "For the earth bringeth fruit of herself; first the blade, then the ear, after that the full corn in the ear." Success requires effort, just as a goal can't be achieved without journeying through the process.

Take pregnancy, for example. It lasts 37 to 40 weeks, no matter the prayer and fasting; labor before 37 weeks is called preterm, and rushing the gestation process could risk complications for both mother and child. The waiting period is for growth and nourishment, preparing for the arrival of new life.

We should choose to focus on the purpose of our pain rather than just its discomfort. Is there something it's intended to remove, introduce, or create? While it's not easy—especially when it feels like a delay or detour—as Christine Caine, an Australian Evangelist, said, "Sometimes when you are in a dark place, you may feel you have been buried, when in fact you have been planted."

We are bound by laws and processes that govern our lives; faith does not exempt us from these steps. No matter how much we love our children, we don't give them a car at the age of three because we want them to have great things in life. We wait until they are of age to take responsibility for the blessing (1 Corinthians 13:11). Just as a child must grow through stages of development, Jesus Himself was not exempt from this process. Even though Jesus Christ was fully God and had been slain before the foundations of the world were laid (Revelation 13:8), Jesus still had to be born by a woman, and He learned the scriptures. He experienced challenges- he lost a friend, was betrayed, was forsaken by the disciples, was persecuted, and was crucified despite being the Son of God. He needed to die so that the Scriptures may be fulfilled. He showed us that there is no glory without process—no greatness without overcoming difficulties.

Some have left the faith because of incomplete or incorrect teachings that promise a life free from challenges. However, salvation doesn't eliminate our responsibility for growth. We must work out our salvation daily (Philippians 2:12), with gradual transformation from within. We will face trials, but these trials don't destroy us; they refine us, just as fire transforms gold (Isaiah 43:2). Situations may try to diminish our hope and faith; however, we are encouraged by the words: "We have this treasure in earthen vessels, that the excellence of the power may be of God and not of us. We are hard-pressed on every side, yet not crushed; we are perplexed, but not in despair; persecuted, but not forsaken; struck down, but not destroyed" (2 Corinthians 4:7–9).

Like Abraham, who waited 25 years for God's promise, we, too, may find ourselves in a season of process. However, this waiting prepares us for what lies ahead. Ultimately, Abraham became the father of many nations (Hebrews 6:15). Similarly,

God tests and prepares us, making it unwise to judge situations or people we do not fully understand. **Just as plants have different germination times and meals require different cooking durations, it is inadvisable to criticize or compare individuals; each person's journey is unique.**

Embrace your scars, for they often reveal the growth and strength that come from overcoming challenges. No wonder Apostle Joshua Selman, founder and senior pastor of Eternity Network International, states, "Never hide your scars, as there may come a time when your scar could be the key to a specific opportunity."

THE BIG PICTURE

To understand the big picture of our lives, we need to discover the Creator's intentions when He made us. Just like manufacturers usually have a need in mind before making a product to meet the demand. Using the product for a purpose other than its intended use may cause malfunction. Products typically come with a manual that explains the product and its functions.

Similarly, we were born for a reason and a season, requiring our choices to be fulfilled. We were given a manual, the Bible, and the Spirit of God to help us understand our gifts, talents, and functions, enabling us to achieve maximum productivity.

For we are His workmanship [His own master work, a work of art], created in Christ Jesus [reborn from above—spiritually transformed, renewed, ready to be used] for good works, which God prepared [for us] beforehand [taking paths which He set], so that we would walk in them [living the good life which He prearranged and made ready for us]. (Ephesians 2:10 AMP)

Our predetermined purpose shapes both our environment and our experiences. These experiences are specific to our purpose and destiny, much like Jesus', who died as a sacrifice for our sins. This was the primary reason for His coming to earth. He gave His life to offer free redemption and salvation to all.

The purpose of our existence defines who we are and who we are meant to be. God has a specific plan, purpose, and place for each of us in His overarching program. As Olajumoke Adenowo stated, "Purpose is God's idea, not merely a human opinion; it is the reason for your very existence." Your form is not a mistake; it was created to align with God's intent."

God is the master planner of our lives, much like a movie director who knows the movie's ending. God is not shocked by what happens to us. He works from the end to the beginning as the Alpha and Omega. Everything leads to the divine's expectant end.

"Before I formed you in the womb I knew you; Before you were born I sanctified you; I ordained you a prophet to the nations" (Jeremiah 1:5). Whatever you're going through is not always unto death but for the glory of God.

Your emotional challenge is not to destroy you, although it may feel that way, especially at that time. Just like how an olive is crushed to release its oil, emotional pain can also be the catalyst that unleashes the best in us. Don't let challenges hold you back. Instead, use them as opportunities to rise above and reveal your true potential. **Not all setbacks are necessarily bad for you; some are here to spring you forward.** Setbacks can either distract or redirect you.

Several problems and chaos may arise when there is a mismatch or misalignment between God's plans and ours (Isaiah 55:8). However, not every suffering is a result of what you did wrong, as illustrated in the Biblical story of Job (Job 1–42) where God bragged about Job to the devil. As part of a larger divine plan, Job suffered as a righteous man; he lost everything (children, possessions, and esteem) and was afflicted with painful body sores except for his wife. Ultimately, God restored everything Job had lost.

Similarly, in John 9:1–3, the disciples wondered if the man was born blind because of his parents' sin or his own. Unlike humans who assume all sufferings are sin-related, Jesus clarified that neither the man nor his parents sinned, but the man was born blind, so the works of God should be revealed in him.

Regardless of your faith status, it's crucial to recognize that just because something is God's will doesn't always mean it will be painless or not challenging. Sometimes, challenges serve as proof that we are alive on Earth. God's will doesn't promise an absence of pain, but it does guarantee His presence to be with you and help you through it.

We are encouraged to acknowledge and not deny our emotions, as they make us human while living in the consciousness of God's perspective. Jesus modeled this while He was on earth.

Jesus wept when He learned that His friend Lazarus had passed away. Despite knowing that He would soon raise Lazarus from the dead, Jesus still felt the pain of the loss. This event was intended to bring glory to God (John 11:33–37).

Jesus also felt the pain of betrayal and loneliness: 'And He began to be sorrowful and deeply distressed. Then, He said to them, "My soul is exceedingly sorrowful, even to death. Stay here and watch with Me."'

PRODUCTIVE ISOLATION

Unhealed psychological pain can lead to isolation, which may result in either redirection or stagnation, depending on how we choose to respond to it. This pain can cause us to distance ourselves from loved ones, including God. It's important not to confuse God's silence with His absence. Using this season productively can foster character building and maturity, leading to the fruit of the Holy Spirit. Our dependence on the knowledge and understanding of God's nature can provide comfort as we navigate this period with a perspective beyond our own (Proverbs 3:5).

Many Christians may find the waiting period the most challenging season of their lives. However, this period is not merely a test but also an opportunity for growth and a deeper faith—a time filled with anticipation and hope. Just as germination requires specific conditions such as the right temperature, moisture, and light or darkness, our personal growth requires different factors, including the necessity of isolation at times.

Understanding when to isolate and when to socialize is crucial for our development.

If you abort the challenging season, you will also abort the growth, hindering your self-actualization. **Don't let a temporary setback prevent you from achieving your full potential.** It's essential to keep pushing forward and learn to be comfortable, even when you feel uncomfortable, while trusting the transformative journey. Remember that God is more interested in your personal growth than your short-lived happiness.

Ask any great person, and you will often hear about the cost and sacrifices that accompany greatness. True greatness cannot exist without sacrifice. Without pain, there is no gain. If we bypass the challenging processes, we risk becoming proud and arrogant. Failing to appreciate our experiences may lead us to minimize the grace and mercy of God in our lives (Romans 9:16).

Greatness achieved without sacrifice rarely leads to sustained significance and impact. **No experience is**

wasted; it is all about how you choose to utilize it. You are not behind; you are being prepared.

Discomfort and emotional pain are essential for growth. You were not a mistake but intentionally created to fulfill a purpose (Psalms 139:16, The Message).

POINTERS TO PURPOSE

Psychological pain can be a powerful motivator, urging us to discover our purpose, passions, and unique gifts, thereby glorifying God. Often, at the intersection of pain and passion, life experiences may compel us, with God's help, to recognize, develop, and utilize our talents for personal growth (Proverbs 25:2).

I have found the individual adaptation of the standard analytical tool, SWOT, to be helpful for myself and several people I have recommended it to, including clients, patients, and audience members. This tool analyzes our **S**trengths, **W**eaknesses, **O**pportunities, and **T**hreats. It encourages a critical assessment of our strengths, which can be maximized by recognizing our opportunities and identifying potential threats to our growth and development. This self-reflection can serve as a foundation for uncovering our purpose.

Our interests, gifts, and passions are all indicators of our purpose. By discovering, developing, and deploying these inherent abilities, we gain a significant advantage in fulfilling our purpose. Sometimes, pain and suffering become fertile ground for personal growth. For example, a disability may seem like a limitation, but when understood as a different ability, it can lead to a unique purpose that serves others.

We give meaning to our experiences by linking them to a greater purpose. Your experiences aren't random—they are vital pieces of a larger puzzle that contribute to your destiny. By connecting these experiences, you gain clarity and insight, enabling you to unlock your full potential. Don't let your experiences go to waste—use them to uncover your true purpose.

You may have inherited generational pain or experienced the tragedy of a faulty foundation that affected the expression of your gifts. Perhaps you were bullied for being unique, forced to do things beyond your years, or discouraged by loved ones. Perhaps your enthusiasm was crushed, resulting in low self-esteem. These experiences are part of your journey but don't define you. When connected to your larger purpose, they serve as stepping stones that help you rise and achieve lasting significance.

Our creator's awareness and the blessings of our unique gifts should guide us to be more intentional in pursuing purpose and making a positive impact. These gifts are meant to serve others—not just ourselves. It is not surprising that research shows a connection between having a higher purpose in life and lower risks of mental disorders and suicidal thoughts in U.S. veterans.[1]

According to *The New York Times*, "Only about 25% of American adults know what makes their life meaningful, and

40% either claim neutrality or say they don't know their purpose."[2]

Studies consistently show that knowing your purpose leads to a greater sense of direction, meaning in past and present experiences, improved physical and mental health with a lower incidence of chronic conditions, reduced risk of dementia, fewer disabilities, better sleep, and increased longevity. People who understand their purpose often prioritize preventive health services.[3]

In fact, meaning-centered group psychotherapy (MCGP), compared to support-focused group psychotherapy, has been found to be an effective treatment for psychological, existential, or spiritual distress in patients with advanced cancer.[4]

Finding your purpose can be challenging without first seeking and knowing God, the Creator. Through understanding who He is and following His guidance, we can learn what He created us for and who He has called us to serve. **Without understanding the "WHY" behind our existence, we cannot fully grasp "HOW" to fulfill our purpose.**

GENERATIONAL PURPOSE

Perhaps the hardship you're facing is part of your role as a generational cycle breaker—someone who prevents damage, protects future generations, and blocks the devil's access to your children and descendants. The enemy often targets key individuals, such as fathers, Mothers, and children (Zechariah 13:7).

When God gives you a vision, it's never just for you; it transcends your generation and builds a lasting legacy. Your purpose should outlive you. How you bring that vision to life will determine its growth and impact. But here's the truth: the devil doesn't just sit back and watch. He often attacks where you are most significant. Opposition to great ideas often signals how powerful and impactful they are.

Consider Moses, who was born under a decree to kill all male infants. This was no coincidence. A similar decree was issued during Jesus's time. Both Moses and Jesus were deliverers, and where there is a calling to greatness, opposition rises. Haman opposed Queen Esther, Jezebel came against Elijah, and Sanballat and Tobiah resisted Nehemiah. Great leaders and visionaries face significant opposition.

As Reverend Kayode Tadese, Senior Pastor of Abundant Life International Church, wisely said, "Principalities work in personalities." The key is not to focus solely on the person but to understand that the enemy often works through them. Both God and the devil are in the details. Pay attention to the spiritual forces at work behind the scenes. Recognizing these patterns in your life can reveal the next steps in your journey.

Remember, all grace to achieve and sustain anything comes from above—whether Christian or non-Christian (John 3:27, Psalm 127:1). God trains us for one another, empowering us to uplift and bless others. He transforms us into agents of change in the world. There's no purpose in anything that ends with us; our blessings are meant to be shared with others.

While suffering may seem unbearable at the moment, remember that seeking support from God and others can bring comfort (2 Corinthians 1:3–5). A Yoruba proverb from Nigeria states, "Ile Oba to jo na, ewa lo bu si," which translates to, "When a king's palace burns down, the rebuilt palace is even more beautiful." The most outstanding achievements often emerge from overcoming life's most challenging obstacles.

Invite God into your pain. Even when you don't understand it, He can bring meaning and hope to your experiences, leading you toward healing and wholeness. As Matthew 5:4 (The Message) states, "You're blessed when you feel you've lost what is most dear to you." Only then can you be embraced by the One most dear to you."

Embrace His unconditional love and hope today. He walks with us. A life without Christ is filled with crisis, chaos, and ongoing confusion.

Is there a situation or area in your life where you must trust that God is in the details? Write in your workbook.

Maybe you already have or wish to have Jesus' love in your heart and understand your pain better, but you still seek the next steps for intentional living. Turn to the following pages for additional strategies.

CHAPTER EIGHT

POWER OF WORDS AND BIBLICAL MEDITATION

A man's stomach shall be satisfied from the fruit of his mouth; From the produce of his lips, he shall be filled. Death and life are in the power of the tongue, And those who love it will eat its fruit.

— PROVERBS 18:20-21

Doctor, "I feel useless. My parents said I was good for nothing. Is there hope for me?" "I was teased and bullied through childhood; I'm stuck on those words and cannot pursue my interests; I need help." I was criticized on social media for the post I shared. I deleted my account, but I continue to struggle in other areas. What do I do?" "I can't help but say unkind words to my spouse, my children, my family, and friends; I fear we would divorce. Help!" "I said something mean to my peer, and now, our *communication is awkward. How can I restore that relationship?"*

It's essential to regularly review and evaluate the words we receive from others and the words we speak into our own lives and the lives of those around us as they reflect and shape our minds, thoughts, and feelings.

Our words reflect who we are. The words of a bitter heart are usually angry and damaging (Luke 6:45). We speak from our thoughts and feelings. This is one reason we must assess what comes out of our mouths to ourselves and others and what we allow others to speak into our lives.

Words hold tremendous power. They can inspire, motivate, and encourage people to take action. According to Merriam-Webster, a word is not just a collection of letters but an expression of our thoughts, feelings, and beliefs. It can be a promise, a declaration, and a manifestation of God's will. Therefore, it's important to choose our words carefully and use them wisely, for they have the power to shape our world and impact the lives of those around us.

There is verbal and nonverbal communication. Nonverbal communication doesn't involve words but body language, gestures, and silence. Verbal communication uses words and involves several interconnected areas of our brain and body to execute those words. Our brain, body, soul, and spirit receive signals or messages from the external world and internalize them to produce a response. Words heard through your ears, read through your eyes, received in your heart, and spoken with your mouth are very important as they shape who you are or become.

Many people believe in the power of vision boards, written goals, and plans that guide and shape them. We make confessions, affirmations, and declarations with our words. Have you ever wondered how what you said the other day came to pass? Our words have a profound impact on our thoughts, feelings, and actions.

Our salvation in Jesus Christ begins with confessing with our mouths and believing with our hearts (Romans 10:9). As we've read in previous chapters, we are spirit beings with souls placed in bodies to function on earth. We cannot afford to be careless with our words because we are made in God's image. We carry God's DNA and the power that builds or breaks.

OUR WORDS REFLECT WHO WE ARE AND SHAPE WHO WE BECOME.

Too often, parents and caregivers choose names or speak hurtful words to their children based on their own emotions, unaware that these words can shape their children's personalities, life journeys, and experiences.

Several examples in the Bible of people with names whose lives reflected the meaning of their names are Jabez (borne in pain), Abram (exalted Father) changed by God to Abraham (Father of many nations), Sarai (Princess) changed by God to Sarah (Mother of princes, Hosea (Salvation) changed to

Joshua (God delivers), and Jesus (Savior). Even Jacob, whose name meant "supplanter," lived according to his name, deceiving his brother Esau (Genesis 25:26).

I wish people would have Moses' experience. Pharaoh's daughter named him "Moses," which means "to draw out," without realizing it would align with his upcoming redemptive destiny involving drawing the Israelites out of slavery (Exodus 2:8–10).

It's no wonder some countries are mindful of the names they give their children. For example, in Nigeria, where I was born and raised, names often carry meanings that are often reflected throughout the child's life. Shocking? Every time a name is called, we declare something unseen into existence. Common themes in Nigeria include wealth, God, the king's crown, joy, wonders, and peace, among others.

We should be mindful of names and nicknames. If they don't have a good meaning, I suggest turning them into ones that are tied to God's purpose.

Calling a child "stupid," "cursed," "good for nothing," or saying "you should have been aborted" doesn't add any shade of positivity to that child; instead, these negative words create significant challenges in that child's life to bring these negative words to pass.

Some children struggle with low esteem and identity confusion due to emotional and verbal abuse by family members or bullies. Since our words shape our beliefs, after hearing them multiple times, we tend to believe them, especially if they come from trusted individuals, because we begin to think that they may be the truth.

The CDC categorizes verbal or emotional abuse as an adverse childhood experience that affects about 11 percent of children. Research shows that between 50 and 80 percent of adults may experience emotional abuse in their lifetime. Verbal or emotional abuse may not leave visible scars.

Still, they leave a lasting and damaging effect on the life of a child, who may never be able to complete projects, lack self-confidence in their abilities or skills, be unable to advocate for themselves, feel like a shadow of themselves, feel inferior, make poor decisions, and struggle to attain any positive heights.

Words shape children's thoughts, feelings, and actions; they make up who they are. Children struggle to separate failed events from themselves, seeing themselves as failures. If not dealt with, this can cause a cycle of pain, bitterness, and, perhaps, generational emotional torture.

Similarly, if you call your spouse a useless husband or wife, guess what? That is what they shall become! Don't get me wrong. I know people are imperfect and have weaknesses; however, you should never use hurtful words to describe yourself or others. Perhaps that is how you feel about yourself. Remember, your words also reflect who you are.

We possess creative power akin to God's due to our spiritual heritage. Our belief or disbelief doesn't change this. Weeds grow on land whether a farmer plants seeds or not. However, being believers makes us aware of this and encourages us to be intentional, like God, rather than leaving life or things to chance.

We should be careful and intentional about our jokes. As we have read, we need to seek emotional healing so that we don't hurt others and ourselves because we are hurting. It's never an acceptable excuse. We should also be careful of the words we declare in our lives and environment.

Do you have naysayers around you who wonder if anything good can come from you? Jesus had a similar experience (John 1:46) but didn't stop there. He didn't let the naysayers distract Him from His goal and purpose.

Accept today that you will always have naysayers who are either bitter, ignorant, or jealous. But don't focus on trying to prove anything to them. Let your results speak. Be the best version of yourself by being authentic and growth-focused.

YOU BECOME THE WORD YOU FOCUS ON.

Sometimes, we become the words used about us because we have dwelled on them so much that they begin to shape our lives, thus confirming the doubts, low self-esteem, and negative beliefs others may have about us. By doing this, we let their opinions define us.

Everyone has the right to their opinions, but no opinion should be considered valid without your consent. You can choose whose opinion matters in your life, but it's the opinion of your creator, combined with your own, that should matter the most. Ensure your words align with God's words for your life. Shift your focus from distractions to goals and steps that align with your purpose.

EFFECTIVE COMMUNICATION

"There is one who speaks like the piercings of a sword, But the tongue of the wise promotes health" (Proverbs 12:18).

The role of our tongues in communication is vital as it helps with the articulation of words, the intentions, and the overall impact of our messages. This significance has led to research focused on enhancing communication abilities. For example, a tongue-computer interface has been developed, allowing people with impaired upper body movement to control computers without using their hands."[1]

The Bible teaches that the ability to control our tongues is correlated with the level of wisdom and self-control we possess. The most remarkable aspect of the tongue, above all our body parts, is that it's untamable by a human (James 3:6–12). The fact that our tongues can't be tamed may explain why we sometimes say things we don't mean.

If our words tear others and ourselves down, they align with worldly, unspiritual, and ungodly wisdom stemming from selfish ambition and envy (James 3:15–16). Unfortunately, the world, including social media and TV, encourages cursing and attitudes that divide and promote hatred. Such words and attitudes don't edify, enlighten, or uplift.

Wise speech aligns with God's purposes, and it's for the good of others. Some words are beneficial to us, while others are misleading. We sometimes lie to ourselves or others to make us feel good. Wise words keep us out of trouble (Proverbs 21:23). Wise words are for edification and improvement, not destruction. This includes

giving and receiving feedback, as well as conflict resolution.

Feedback should be constructive and growth-focused rather than destructive or damaging. Can you recall a time when someone said something hurtful to you? How did you receive it? How do you think people receive your mean words? **Don't say it if it will destroy self-esteem—yours and others.**

It's essential to learn the skill of effective communication, which involves active listening, empathy, and nonverbal and verbal communication. We should all strive to be effective communicators. This is a skill I'm still learning. I used to be very blunt with my words. I ignored the impact of my words on the receiver and focused more on my intention. I have learned that we are quick to judge others based on the effects of their actions on us, but we tend to judge ourselves based on our intentions. We are quick to excuse our actions.

A self-aware person who aspires to greatness should be able to conduct critical self-analysis to acknowledge the truth about their impact on themselves or others. Suppose your words and deeds have a consistent intention but an inconsistent impact. In that case, you should consider taking courses and training in effective communication, in addition to asking God for help and apologizing to those you have hurt. Most importantly, look inward. Maybe it's the way you treat and talk to yourself.

Managing our emotions is one way to develop effective communication. Since we only give what we have, we need to consider more thoughtful ways to treat ourselves and others with the same intention. I have learned that there are many ways to express the same idea. For example, there are several ways to say *No*. Sometimes, *No* is sufficient as a complete sentence.

Effective communication is a learnable skill; it involves being mindful of the content, tone, and timing of our words. There is no productive collaboration or partnership without curiosity, communication, courage, connection, and empathy.

Research has shown that a lack of effective communication is one of the top reasons for divorce. Effective communication is one of the most valuable skills that most employers seek, as it helps boost self-esteem.

GIGO

Our thoughts flow from the content of our mental storage, and like the central processing unit in our computers, incorrect or poor-quality input will always produce poor output: "Garbage in, Garbage out." The words we allow can affect the quality of the input and output of our hearts.

> *"For out of the abundance of the heart, the mouth speaks. A good man out of the good treasure of his*

heart brings forth good things, and an evil man out of the evil treasure brings forth evil things. For by your words you will be justified, and by your words you will be condemned."

— (MATTHEW 12:34,35,37)

Good and upright people will produce good fruit from the virtue stored in their hearts. Likewise, out of the evil hidden in their hearts, evil ones will make what is evil. The overflow of what is in your heart will be evident in your actions and discernible in your words.

Our experiences impact the functioning and nature of our hearts not only positively or negatively but also by the quality of words we allow into our ears, see with our eyes, and speak from our mouths. Negative words can harden our hearts, thus ridding them of a godly, teachable, and malleable nature.

Similarly, research, although limited, has shown that in addition to environmental factors such as water, humidity, temperature, nutrition, and light, these types of words can affect the growth of plants. One plant grew when exposed to positive and encouraging words, and the other plant didn't grow when exposed to negative and discouraging words.[2]

What words do you put into your heart knowingly or unknowingly? Is your heart filled with hatred, discord, jealousy, fits of rage, selfish ambition, dissensions, factions, and envy? How can the quality of the input and output be improved?

THE BIBLE

The Bible is a complete guide for every situation. There is a scripture for every emotional concern (II Timothy 3:16–17 AMP).

The Bible is the only active book. It's a living, breathing thing intentionally designed to meet our daily needs. The Bible doesn't agree with everything we do, but it reveals who we are to ourselves and helps us achieve spiritual maturity that transcends every area of our lives.

> *For the Word that God speaks is alive and full of power [making it active, operative, energizing, and effective]; it is sharper than any two-edged sword, penetrating to the dividing line of the breath of life (soul) and [the immortal] spirit, and of joints and marrow [of the deepest parts of our nature], exposing and sifting and analyzing and judging the very thoughts and purposes of the heart. And not a creature exists that is concealed from His sight, but all things are open and exposed, naked and defenseless to the eyes of Him with Whom we have to do.*
>
> — (HEBREWS 4:12–13 AMPC)

The Bible is different from other books. It's about God—His character, ways, and power revealed directly by Himself, His Son, and His Spirit. The Bible tells us everything we need to navigate this world's rollercoaster.

You cannot truly survive with a lasting effect without a superior advantage, knowledge, or assistance. Chaos doesn't respond to our tears or complaints but to God's Word. We shouldn't be surprised when darkness comes (Genesis 1:1–3). Still, rather than wallow in tears, we should declare His specific word to restore order in every chaos (Job 22:28).

PROMISES

We should not be ignorant of God's promises and the associated activating conditions so that people and the devil won't cheat us. God didn't say **if** these troubles would come, but remember that He is with you **when** they come. We have been empowered to face obstacles. Guess what! The devil knows this, too, so he strikes before we realize who we are in God; the devil takes advantage of our ignorance, doubts, or confusion.

The Bible contains promises based on conditions that we often overlook or don't commonly consider. According to the Merriam-Webster dictionary, a promise is "a declaration that one will do or refrain from doing something specified."

We are often quick to claim a promise without fully understanding the requirements or the process it entails. Several promises are based on our obedience and submission to God. Some are based on universal principles that apply to all, including non-believers, such as the laws of sowing and reaping and the laws of times and seasons.

POWER OF WORDS AND BIBLICAL MEDITATION

In partnership with our faith, all promises are fulfilled according to His will (I John 5:14). While we doubt some promises because we don't fully believe them, we often receive what we believe rather than what we ask for.

Unfortunately, your experience may lead you to doubt God's Word due to a lack of trust or a poor understanding of His words. It's essential to know God's character before using His words. God has integrity and ability.

A spoken word is essential, but the one who speaks the word is even more critical because of the presence or lack of integrity and the ability to act according to the Word. God is bound by His words.

So will My word be which goes out of My mouth; It will not return to Me void (useless, without result), Without accomplishing what I desire, And without succeeding in the matter for which I sent it.

— (ISAIAH 55:11)

BIBLE READING

This Book of the Law shall not depart from your mouth, but you shall meditate in it day and night, that you may observe to do according to all that is written in it. For then you will make your way prosperous, and then you will have good success.

— (JOSHUA 1:8)

Reading, in general, has been shown to improve brain and mental health. It enhances brain connectivity, reduces depressive symptoms, prevents cognitive decline, improves physical health by lowering blood pressure and heart rate, and promotes better sleep. It also enhances vocabulary and comprehension. These benefits are also seen in Bible reading, which can improve our word storage as we function like God on earth.

Dr. Michael Ferguson, an investigator at the Center for Brain Circuit Therapeutics at Brigham and Women's Hospital in Boston, MA, USA, performed a study that revealed that three brain regions were mainly activated when engaging in spiritual activities such as prayer and reading the Bible: the medial prefrontal cortex, frontal lobe, and nucleus accumbens.

These are regions of the brain responsible for cognitive thinking, behavior, and reward systems. They contribute to changing our beliefs and have a lasting impact on our thoughts and behaviors. Dopamine, a neurotransmitter associated with the reward system, plays a crucial role in focus, motivation, and maintaining a happy mood. Dopamine was found to be released while reading the Bible.[3] Additionally, the reward system is crucial in regulating addiction.

Dopamine affects our cognition, thoughts, and mood. Reading the Bible impacts neural pathways that affect our cognitive processes and behavior and has been found to reduce rates of loneliness, anger, substance use, bitterness, gambling, sexual immorality, etc.

This highlights the importance of reading the Bible in a manner that positively impacts our brain, body, soul, and spirit. These are affected by the words we hear through our ears, read through our eyes, receive in our hearts, and speak with our mouths, thus contributing to our character.

God's Word is a strong foundation of our faith and relationship with God. The more we meditate on God's Word, the more of God is in us. We change from being self-centered people to God-pleasing people.

BIBLICAL MEDITATION

According to Merriam-Webster's dictionary, meditation is defined as "close or continued thought; the turning or revolving of a subject in the mind; serious contemplation." The word meditation is used in several religions, including Christianity. While there are diverse meditation practices, the end goal is the same: mindfulness.

Non-biblical meditation is a popular and evidence-based mind-body exercise in psychology. It has its roots in Buddhism and is primarily focused on detachment from the world to cultivate a deeper understanding of the self. By promoting mind-body integration and well-being, it's often recommended to reduce or eliminate worry, stress, emotional fatigue, depression, and anxiety disorders.

Research has found meditation to be helpful for several medical disorders when combined with conventional medicine.

Biblical meditation is a reflective process that involves contemplation of the Scriptures. It focuses on detaching from worldly distractions to cultivate deeper connections with God for personal transformation and spiritual maturity. We don't only empty ourselves of the world as seen in non-biblical meditation; we fill our minds with God's Words instead of ourselves.

As we consistently meditate on the Scriptures, our logical center (prefrontal cortex) and emotions (limbic system) align and gradually transform into a better version of ourselves—the God-intended version. Eventually, we will be more mindful, thoughtful, and intentional in our speech.

Transformation requires God's Word, which equips us; prayer, which empowers us; and God's Spirit, who leads and strengthens us. The necessary transformation is incomplete if it's not reflected in our minds, hearts, wills, and emotions, which comprise the soul. Transformation involves filling our minds with God's love and words until we become like Jesus.

Biblical meditation requires intelligent engagement with our senses: reading, hearing, speaking, studying, and memorizing the Scriptures. Biblical medication can heal our hearts, renew our minds, and remove harmful and unproductive thoughts with the help of the Spirit of God.

If we don't believe God's Words, our brain may resist them as lies. However, it's essential to understand that faith is not about believing in a lie; instead, it's about being aware of what is seen and trusting in something beyond what we can see or understand.

Hebrews 11:1 AMP beautifully states, "Faith is the evidence of things not seen and the conviction of their reality—faith comprehends as fact what cannot be experienced by the physical senses."

Biblical meditation is a powerful technique for internalizing God's Word. It involves actively moving the word from mere information to a state of consciousness and awareness in our imagination and thoughts. It's crucial to understand that imagination is impossible without visualizing with our minds. We must actively visualize God's Words in our minds.

Ingesting God's Word is like consuming food that becomes part of our digestive system, contributing to our growth and productivity. As we become one with God's Word, it transforms us from a state of doubt to hope and expectation, building our faith in God's power.

Studying, listening, and confessing God's Word will fill our minds and thoughts. The more we have God's Word in us, the more of God's power and strength we have within us (Ephesians 3:20).

Remember, during rough times, the Holy Spirit brings timely and relevant scriptures to remembrance. **Your word storage and library are vital.** While Jesus was on earth, He repeatedly said, "It is written," and quoted scriptures to overcome situations.

The Holy Spirit also aids in understanding and revealing God's words in various situations (John 15:26, Job 32:8). Otherwise, these words lack power (2 Corinthians 3:6). Your class, caliber, and gender don't influence how well you comprehend God's Word. And it's certainly not by how religious, intelligent, or educated you are (Isaiah 29:11–12, Acts 8:30–32). "But the natural man does not receive the things of the Spirit of God, for they are foolishness to him; nor can he know *them* because they are spiritually discerned" (2 Corinthians 2:14).

Do you better understand how to use your words but wonder how to use them to communicate more effectively with God and others? Then flip the page to the next chapter for some insight.

CHAPTER NINE

THE DYNAMIC PURPOSE OF PRAYER

Men should always pray and not lose heart.

— LUKE 18:1

Doctor! "How do I deal with my struggle to have faith or believe in the place of prayer with my history of abuse and emotional challenges?" "How can I talk to God after He has let me down?" "How can I focus when I want to talk to God?" "How can I trust God for anything?" "Can I combine prayer with therapy?"

I can empathize with you regarding your emotional struggle. Perhaps the concept of God remains foreign to you. I applaud your curiosity.

What comes to your mind as you hear the word "prayer"? Do you see prayer as a chore, a complicated thing, a waste of time, or a one-sided communication? Does it feel like talking to someone you are not sure exists or listens? Is it just a religious activity? Do you pray out of compulsion or obligation?

WHAT IS PRAYER?

Prayer is simply communicating or speaking with God as our Father. Communication is an exchange of information. Prayer is a two-way communication between God and humanity, rooted in a relationship. Imagine prayer as a form of communication akin to sending emails, text messages, or making phone calls to God. Prayer to God is spurred by dependence, love, intimacy, and connection.

God invited us to pray for our own sake, not His own. Without prayer, we suggest we are self-sufficient and don't need God's help. **Prayer may start solely focused on our needs but must not remain transactional.**

How would you feel if someone approached you only when they needed something, and after sharing their needs, they left and moved on to other things, as if you didn't exist? If that person were an adult, you might consider them a user.

Babies primarily focus on their basic needs, including food, security, and regular diaper changes. These needs change as a child grows, perhaps to say, "Hello, Daddy or Mommy, how are you?"

The relationship eventually evolves from a one-sided, need-focused relationship to a dialogue of communication that fosters a deeper connection between the parent or caregiver and the child. A young child focuses on needs, and a mature child focuses on relationships.

Our relationship with God may start as a provider-child relationship. Still, as our approach to caregiving evolves, both physically and emotionally, our relationship with God should deepen and become more akin to a father-child relationship. Our relationship with God should grow as we progress through stages and phases, ultimately becoming dependable as heirs to handle His fatherly, Godly responsibilities.

Prayer should focus on building relationships with intimacy and knowledge of one another, the exact requirements of building any human relationship. Building a quality relationship requires investing time and effort.

We often label someone as selfish or a user when they prioritize their interests for convenience. This behavior can lead to frustration in our relationships. Our pain can make us selfish, causing us to want things on our terms, and as a result, we may become manipulative. No one likes to feel used.

GOD'S NATURE

Often, we project our experiences from our relationship with our earthly parents or caregivers onto God. For example, if your father is strict, yells at you, criticizes you, condemns you, abuses or is not trustworthy, you may tend to think God is this way too.

Such thought processes strain and ruin our relationship with God because of our distorted perception of Him. God is our Heavenly Father, not human (Numbers 23:19). Understanding God's nature and character is essential to distinguish God from humanity.

God doesn't have mood swings that impact when He hears us. He doesn't love like human beings love. God loves us unconditionally. We have sonship status through His son, Jesus Christ. We must understand this; it can alter how we perceive and relate to God, as well as our understanding of our challenges. "But God clearly shows *and* proves His own love for us, by the fact that while we were still sinners, Christ died for us" (Romans 5:8).

God doesn't get overwhelmed by our prayers, take a break, or send our prayers to voicemail. **We don't bother or inconvenience God. We don't have to take turns praying to God. We're not in a queue to pray.** God doesn't tell us to return later because He is too busy with other things.

He is not a human being who cannot multitask effectively and efficiently.

God is our Heavenly Father, who is all-sufficient, Omnipresent (everywhere), omniscient (all-knowing), and omnipotent (all-powerful). These are some of the many features that make Him God, not just a superhuman or an ideology.

God doesn't consider our prayer points unimportant or categorize our prayer as small versus big. He loves honesty and sincerity. He is touched by our emotions but responds to His words, including His principles and promises. He is sovereign and Almighty, yet He remains approachable.

Some pray to God as strangers, babes, and others as mature children. What is the status of your relationship with Him?

SCIENCE OF PRAYER

Over many decades, prayer has been challenging to study for multiple reasons. Many researchers are skeptical about religious beliefs. It's challenging to rely solely on subjective reports, as there are various prayer styles and reasons for prayer. Additionally, scientists are unable to study God's involvement during prayer.

Several neuroscientists have observed multiple brain scans of those who pray and meditate. They noticed increased activity in the frontal lobes, which are linked to attention and focus, and reduced activity in specific brain areas, such as the parietal lobe — a region related to our sense of space and time. Prayer has been shown to stimulate the release of serotonin and dopamine, which can lead to a happy mood and increased pleasure, thereby fostering greater engagement in these activities.

Prayer is different from meditation therapy. The former is primarily active, while the latter is passive. Some have described prayer as a form of contemplative meditation, with prayer being a conversation with God and meditation being a process of listening to God.

Prayer can be combined with taking medications and other psychological techniques. Research shows that prayer has psychological benefits similar to meditation, reducing stress and worry. It shuts down one's fight-or-flight response. Prayer directs our focus from our constant worries to God and godly things. Prayer helps with mindfulness.

Several studies have been able to study the effect or outcome of intercessory prayer or prayer in groups, which have shown that prayer caused:[1]

- Significant improvement in psychological well-being
- Improvement in depression
- Increased optimism
- Improvement in anxiety
- Reduction in anger and aggression as prayer can provide a new perspective

Such improvements were observed to be sustained for at least one year in participants who received prayer intervention compared to those who didn't.[2]

Your approach to God matters. Those who approached God as a partner or collaborator had better mental and physical health outcomes. People who were angry at God, who felt punished or abandoned, or who relinquished responsibility and deferred to God for solutions had worse outcomes.[3]

THE DYNAMIC PURPOSE OF PRAYER

PURPOSE OF PRAYER

Relationship

Prayer should flow from a relationship with God, not out of a sense of urgency. God loves us and desires communication with us. Prayer should be a lifestyle (1 Thessalonians 5:17), not just reserved for times of emergency. It's not about *if* we pray, but *when* we pray (Mark 11:24).

The more we fellowship with God, the deeper our relationship becomes. Imagine a parent with a child who never communicates yet demands access to their belongings. We can't claim closeness without communication. Effective communication and investment of time are crucial to any lasting relationship, including the one with God.

Jesus demonstrated sonship by regularly praying, even withdrawing from distractions to be with His Father (Mark 1:35). Despite being fully God and fully man, He prioritized prayer. We should do the same, regardless of how busy life gets. Prayer should come from love, not just need. God is not a genie or magician. The deeper our love for God, the more we'll open up to Him with our concerns without boundaries.

Transformation and renewal

Prayer brings profound change in every area of our lives and helps us align with God's will. "As Jesus was praying, the appearance of His face became different [actually transformed], and His clothing became white and flashing with the brilliance of lightning" (Luke 9:29 AMP).

We often struggle with the idea of change, but change is constant and unavoidable, making us either better or bitter. Prayer helps us surrender and radically accept the guidance and instruction from the One who loves us the most and desires the best for us.

Even when we do everything right and meet all the required conditions, we still have unanswered prayers, perhaps better described as pending answers. Our hope can be delayed or redirected, leading us to question God's existence and abilities.

Submission to God's will can be challenging for even the strongest believers, as seen in Jesus' example in Luke 22:42–44. Since God is our Father who sees and knows everything, we should sincerely acknowledge our feelings during difficult times, but we must not stop there. We should also seek the grace and ministry of angels to strengthen us, just as Jesus did. We can only do everything through Christ, who strengthens us (Philippians 4:13).

Søren Kierkegaard, a Danish theologian, stated, "The function of prayer is not to influence God, but rather to change the nature of the one who prays." While salvation secures our spirit, our minds must be transformed to reflect Christ's likeness in every area of life (Romans 12:2). Transformation is gradual—it doesn't happen overnight. Without transformation, life remains unproductive and stagnant (Ephesians 4:18).

Transformation is achieved by renewing our beliefs and exchanging old perspectives for new ones. Like a computer, old applications must be uninstalled and new ones installed. Prayer is the place of exchange, from selfishness to God-centeredness, from bitterness to joy, from foolishness to wisdom and guidance, and from unrest to peace.

Life's challenges can lead to despair, as seen in Elijah's struggle with depression and suicidal thoughts (1 Kings 19:4). God was not displeased with him. Instead, God provided nourishment and emotional and spiritual support through angels. Jesus, too, experienced distress to the point of death but was strengthened by an angel to continue His mission (Luke 22:43–44).

Prayer first changes us internally before impacting our circumstances. Sustainable change starts within. As Apostle Joshua Selman said, "The journey of renewal and transformation introduces you to the person of the Holy Spirit." The Holy Spirit is the key to true transformation, empowering us with wisdom, guidance, and strength to fulfill God's will (John 14:16–17, Romans 8:4–5). The Holy Spirit is not an "it" but a personality—the powerhouse of God, central to the Trinity.

How will you recognize when the change you seek has occurred if your heart remains unhealed? To change the world, we must first be the change we want to see. Without the Holy Spirit, we are led by worldly desires and sinful nature. He enables us to discern and embrace the things of God (1 Cor 2:14), guiding us to spiritual growth and transformation. Prayer, the Word, and fellowship with the Holy Spirit bring illumination and understanding.

The Holy Spirit transforms our weaknesses into strength, helping us walk in holiness and freedom. He guarantees our relationship with God (Romans 8:14–17). Through His guidance, our pain is turned into power and purpose, allowing us to live out God's calling.

Spiritual matters don't always make sense to the natural mind (1 Corinthians 2:14), but the Holy Spirit empowers us to conceive what seems impossible. Prayer is expected of all, as seen in Luke 18:1. God's Spirit ignites a passion in us to act boldly and with joy. Great men are sustained by their submission to the Holy Spirit.

It's vital to embrace the person of the Holy Spirit. He provides comfort in suffering (John 14:26) and exchanges darkness for light, confusion for clarity, and formlessness for meaning (Genesis 1:1). God specializes in transforming our weaknesses—such as a lack of self-control, condemnation and immorality—into holiness and freedom. Without the Holy Spirit, spiritual practices like prayer, fasting, and Bible reading would be frustrating. He gives us direction, revelation, and the ability to make fruitful decisions. He enables us to fulfill God's will and purpose, leading to transformation (Philippians 2:13).

Through prayer, the ministry of the Word, and fellowship with the Holy Spirit, we gain deeper understanding. The more we allow God into our lives, the more He reveals Himself to us.

How can God transform your weakness, pain, or disappointment into power and purpose? It would take power beyond our intellect and human abilities to cause wonders, including healing and freedom from oppression. The Holy Spirit is the guarantee of our belonging to God (Romans 8:14–17 AMP).

Growth and maturity:
Some Christians prioritize reading the Bible over prayer and vice versa, but both are required for spiritual maturity and transformation. Jesus showed the importance of God's Word, prayer, and empowerment by God's Spirit during His ministry on earth.

After Jesus' empowerment on earth, He was taken to the wilderness, where He fasted for forty days and forty nights for spiritual nourishment and sustenance. He overcame the devil's temptations with God's Word (Matthew 4).

The apostles also demonstrated the importance of this, as they devoted themselves to both prayer and God's Word (Acts 6:4). These are the tools we need to achieve multidimensional maturity in our earthly pursuits and aspirations.

The Bible documents that Jesus grew in stature—physical maturity, wisdom, intellectual maturity, and favor with God—spiritual and relational maturity (Luke 2:52).

Although we have the DNA and potential for greatness, it will not manifest unless we attain the required stature and maturity (Galatians 4:1).

For example, we may have a car willed to us by a loved one, but we won't be legally allowed to drive it unless we learn how to drive and pass the driving test. If we drive it illegally, we risk being arrested or causing accidents and malfunctions.

Prayer helps us develop spiritual stamina and power to fulfill our God-given assignment and purpose of existence. We are assured that there will be troubles as long as we are in this world (John 16:33).

The need to build capacity and character is required for all human beings to survive and thrive in the current and future challenges. "Many *are* the afflictions of the righteous, But the Lord delivers him out of them all" (Psalms 34:19).

A prayerless believer of God is a powerless Christian. Prayer can transform a timid person into a confident and bold individual (Acts 4:13). We need courage to face certain situations and people so we won't miss opportunities or be intimidated by the good things in life. **Committing to healing from trauma and overcoming adversities takes courage and boldness.**

To obtain requests and make petitions:
In prayer, we make our supplications and desires known to God, believing in His abilities. We receive illumination, direction, and guidance about our desires when we pray about our requests (Matthew 7:7–11).

Prayer is the platform where we ask, seek, and find to obtain what God wills. He is not only a prayer-hearing God but also a prayer-answering God.

Our desires must align with His will to receive. God's Spirit only backs up and supports God's will for the glory of God, not according to our intentions or selfish desires.

> *"And this is the confidence that we have in him, that, if we ask anything according to his will, he heareth us:*

and if we know that he hear us, whatsoever we ask, we know that we have the petitions that we desired of him"

— (1 JOHN 5:14–15).

Warfare and intercessions:
We should also pray because we are not alone in this world. Other human beings and demonic influences surround us. Demonic spirits want chaos, confusion, wickedness, and everything that is against God.
The devil is not happy when you're happy. He has come to steal, kill, and destroy (Matthew 10:10). He is described as a roaring lion seeking and looking for whom to devour (I Peter 5:8). Therefore, we cannot afford to be ignorant of the devil's strategies. Since the devil is neither omnipresent nor omniscient, he customizes his tactics and weapons based on knowledge relevant to our profile and situations (Isaiah 54:17). A lack of awareness of this reality could cost us everything in our lives and the lives of those around us.

Put on the whole armor of God so that you may be able to stand against the wiles of the devil. For we do not wrestle against flesh and blood, but against principalities, against powers, against the rulers of the darkness of this age, against spiritual hosts of wickedness in the heavenly places. Therefore take up the whole armor of God, that you may be able to withstand in the evil day, and having done all, to stand.

— (EPHESIANS 6:11–13)

Prayer helps us to rebuke the forces of darkness. There are spirits. Spirits cannot be destroyed, but they can be rebuked from a territory (James 4:7). Demonic influences can be fearful or cause false beliefs in our minds, which paralyze us because things are first created in our minds (Gen 11:5–6). This becomes a significant issue, as it can impact our perspectives and influence our views, leading to limitations and stagnation in our lives and our ability to believe in God's power (Ephesians 3:20).

Prayer helps us cast down these false arguments and take charge of thoughts that don't support God's will, such as fear. Once present, fear opens the door to other forms of negativity.

> *For the weapons of our warfare are not carnal but mighty in God for pulling down strongholds, casting down arguments and every high thing that exalts itself against the knowledge of God, bringing every thought into captivity to the obedience of Christ, and being ready to punish all disobedience when your obedience is fulfilled.*
>
> — (2 CORINTHIANS 10:4–6)

Sometimes, our loved ones, including parents, siblings, friends, spouses, employers, colleagues, etc., can become victims. They are used as weapons of distraction against us, causing destruction or hardship that can affect us.

Since demonic forces can influence personalities to harm or directly influence us to self-destruct (Mark 5: 1–20), praying for ourselves and those around us is critical. We cannot afford to be selfish. What affects your neighbor may eventually affect you (James 5:13–16).

Spiritual legislation:
We pray because we have God's DNA and have been made kings and priests on earth (Revelation 5:10). God has chosen to involve us in establishing His will on earth as it is in Heaven (Psalms 115:16).
Prayer is like the control room of a company or a house, where we legislate and agree with God over the decisions of our lives and territories. "I assure you *and* most solemnly say to you, whatever you bind [forbid, declare to be improper and unlawful] on earth shall have [already] been bound in heaven, and whatever you loose [permit, declare lawful] on earth shall have [already] been loosed in heaven" (Matthew 18:18 AMP). **Prayer is not an option but a necessity for humanity. When we don't pray, evil, disasters, and chaos multiply in our lives and the world.** Apostle Joshua Selman stated, "Prayerlessness is the highest demonstration of pride. It's a declaration of self-sufficiency and independence from the need for God's help. Prayer is not a fruit of the Holy Spirit, like taking your bath daily or working out; you may be tired, but it requires self-discipline."

HOW TO PRAY

Jesus provides a guide in Matthew 6:5–14 of the Bible. Since prayer is communicating with God, our Heavenly Father, here are some things to consider:

Belief system: Your belief in God's existence, character, Word, and abilities determines if, when, and what you receive. We should approach God by first believing He exists (Hebrews 11:6). It would be hard to talk to someone you don't believe exists or trust, someone you think wouldn't listen to you, perhaps someone who has favorites or a God who cannot deliver His promises (Ephesians 3:20).

We receive what we believe in our hearts, not necessarily what we desire or ask. "Whatever things you ask when you pray, believe that you receive them, and you will have them" (Mark 11:24).

If we believe in God and His word, we should pray using His words in the Bible because He honors His word even more than His name (Psalms 138:2). While prayer can aid in submission to God's will, it cannot alter the required conditions for His promises as discussed in Chapter 7. Disobedience or partial obedience may cause self-inflicted delays.

Attentional focus: Have you ever been in a conversation where the other person seems distracted or uninterested? It can be frustrating to feel like you're not being heard or valued, hindering effective communication.

When you pray, it's essential to give your complete attention to God and eliminate any distractions that might come your way. This will help you to connect with Him on a deeper level and enable you to experience the true essence of prayer. Make every communication with God count by focusing solely on Him and seeking quality time over unfocused quantity.

Developing the skill of being present and engaged requires practice, and a clear structure of prayer in place can help improve engagement and maintain focus.

Intention analysis: Is it to please people or to please God? Is it according to His will or yours? (I John 5:14). Do you want him to agree with your decision, or do you want His opinion? Do you want a magician or a genie? "You ask and do not receive, because you ask amiss, that you may spend *it* on your pleasures" (James 4:3).

Prayer is not a tool to do God a favor. Although we may sometimes feel desperate for answers, it is essential to understand that prayer cannot compel God to fulfill our heart's desires. God is not human and doesn't operate according to our preferences or likes. He is a Supreme Being with principles and order; He is GOD.

Attitude and Posture: Are You God-Dependent or Self-Sufficient? Do you diligently seek Him? Do you love Him, or is it more of a ritual? Do you honor or despise Him? Do you read or know His word (Matthew 22:29)? Are you willing to obey His instructions? Are there sins to confess? Are there people we need to forgive? No one can stand if God were to count our sins (Psalms 130:3).

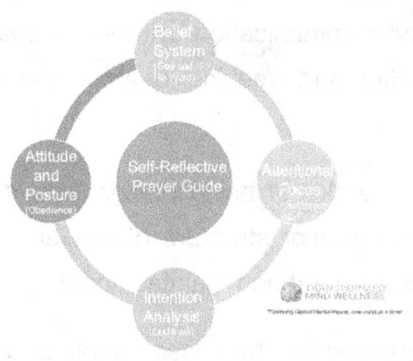

Do you now understand the benefits of prayer better but wonder about additional strategies for generational transformation? Stay tuned and flip to the subsequent pages.

CHAPTER TEN

THE GIFT OF FORGIVENESS

And be kind to one another, tenderhearted, forgiving one another, even as God in Christ forgave you.

— EPHESIANS 4:32

Doctor, *what is the impact of forgiveness on my mental and emotional health? Why does forgiveness matter? Why must I forgive my abusers and those who have hurt me? Some have never recognized the hurt they caused and have never apologized to me. Is forgiveness the same as forgetting the hurt?*

Unforgiveness is often the result of resentment, anger, or bitterness due to a wrong done to us. Maybe abuse, oppression, or embarrassment altered our expectations of the offender, situation, or ourselves. It becomes incredibly challenging when the offender fails to acknowledge or justify the harm. Seeing, speaking to, or hearing about the offender can evoke feelings of anger, disgust, or bitterness.

Sometimes, we find some offenders easier to deal with than others who are more challenging to forgive. However, forgiveness remains an important decision or choice to consider in every relationship. Nelson Mandela, the renowned South African President who fought against apartheid at the expense of his freedom, stated, "Resentment is like drinking poison and then hoping it will kill your enemies."

Nelson Mandela was released on February 11, 1990, after 27 years in prison, having believed that no man was superior to another. Despite the anger and resentment that was triggered by his multiple losses while in prison and immediately after his release, Nelson Mandela stated during his interview with Bill Clinton:

> "*I stayed alive on hate for 12 years. I broke rocks every day, and I stayed alive on hate. They took a lot away from me. They took me away from my wife, and it subsequently destroyed my marriage. They took me away from seeing my children grow up. They abused me mentally and physically. And one day, I realized they could take it all except my mind and heart. Those things I would have to give to them, and I simply decided not to give them away.*"
>
> — *(A MAN CALLED HOPE: BILL CLINTON ON NELSON MANDELA/ VANITY FAIR)*

THE GIFT OF FORGIVENESS

Nelson Mandela united South Africa by focusing on reconciliation and forgiveness to heal the land. He attributed this to God-inspired guidance: 'Then the Spirit of Jesus said to me, "Nelson, while you were in prison, you were free, now that you are free, don't become their prisoner."' His legacy of forgiveness and transformation earned him a Nobel Peace Prize and a yearly celebration of his values is observed on July 18, known as International Nelson Mandela Day.

Forgiveness is not:

- Forgetting what happened
- Excusing, denying, or minimizing the effect of what happened
- Automatically resuming the relationship as though nothing happened
- Avoiding the lessons from the error
- Lack of healthy boundaries

Forgiveness is:

- A commitment to a choice to heal by replacing or changing the evil wishes towards the offender with good desires, for example, replacing anger, bitterness, and hatred with empathy and compassion
- Not excusing the outcome of the wrongdoing
- Getting to a state of not referring to the event with the same level of pain and hurt as though it just happened

- A willingness to grant forgiveness in advance, regardless of the offender's consent or apologies

FORGIVENESS AND HEALING

Forgiveness is a decision; the process of working through it is a form of healing. People often assume they are the same. The healing duration varies from person to person and may also differ from one offense to offense. Without forgiveness, trust cannot be rebuilt.

When you recall past offenses, you may require personal and frequent reminders of your commitment to forgive as part of the ongoing healing process. For example, it's okay to tell yourself for the umpteenth time, "I choose to forgive today."

Forgiveness and healing do not focus on erasing memories from the brain, as they are stored as events. They involve creating new memories around the event, allowing new and positive emotions to develop. Forgetting, in the context of forgiveness, means choosing to focus or dwell less on the hurt and stop replaying the offense.

Despite our efforts over time, many people continue to struggle with the concept of forgiveness. We can only truly forgive others when we recognize the forgiveness we have received for our wrongdoings. As it is written, "A man can receive nothing unless it has been given to him from heaven" (John 3:27).

FORGIVENESS AND HUMANITY

Forgiveness requires a constant awareness of our nature as human beings—fallen, flawed, and imperfect—and gratitude for God's amazing grace and mercy. Without this gift, there would be no good in this dark world. Forgiveness requires humility.

Most of us expect others to forgive our mistakes, but we struggle to do the same for others because we focus on their mistakes. We judge ourselves based on our intentions but judge others by the impact of their actions. We all require forgiveness from God for one thing or another (Psalms 130:3).

Forgiveness is the act of giving up your right to be right or retaliate against an offender. Some people find it difficult to forgive and let go of their resentment towards God for something they believe He did or didn't do. They question whether God saw or understood their pain, and they desire retribution.

Sometimes, we struggle to forgive others because we cannot forgive ourselves. The desire for perfection in our expectations of God, others, and ourselves is rooted in an all-or-nothing mindset, which can be a barrier to receiving forgiveness from God and extending forgiveness to others and ourselves.

We cannot maintain a strategic relationship without forgiveness and tolerance, especially if we still want these relationships. Forgiveness involves the gift of compassion, mercy, and accommodation, which is accepting the behavior with understanding and empathy. Offenses often come from different people (Luke 17:1), and we may also offend others. Joyce Meyer stated, "If someone has offended you, start sowing forgiveness. You may need some yourself someday." Without tolerance and forgiveness, we would cut everybody out of our lives, including God and ourselves.

SELF-UNFORGIVENESS

Are you dealing with personal condemnation?

Personal condemnation can significantly impact how we see the world and everything and everyone in it. Feeling ashamed can be a humbling experience, but it often stems from a sense of pride.

I've seen many of my patients and clients struggle to acknowledge and understand that their feelings of shame and self-blame were holding them back. Once they could let go of these negative emotions and stopped blaming themselves for not knowing better, they experienced a sense of freedom. It was like they could finally move forward and break free from the limitations holding them back.

No wonder Nelson Mandela stated, "Forgiveness liberates the soul; it removes fear. That's why it's such a powerful weapon."

Admit your mistakes and wrongs in humility to God and others (2 Corinthians 5:21). Don't let anyone define you by your mistakes. Everyone has made or will make a mistake.

Making a mistake doesn't make you unique. Your strength lies in how you recover from the error.

Please don't dwell on your mistakes; instead, turn them into lessons, not regrets. Lessons help you grow, but regrets keep you stuck. Learning engages your thinking brain (prefrontal cortex), whereas dwelling on regrets activates your feeling brain (amygdala). Embrace learning to foster personal growth and reduce the emotional weight of regret.

Have you wondered if self-unforgiveness is why you may quickly criticize and condemn others?

Forgiveness of oneself and others is essential because one cannot become great without it. If you want to fly like an eagle or gain speed, you cannot have baggage that weighs you down and prevents or delays you from reaching your destination, your goals, and your purpose.

> *As for us, we have all of these great witnesses who encircle us like clouds. So we must let go of every wound that has pierced us and the sin we so easily fall into. Then, we will be able to run life's marathon race with passion and determination, for the path has been already marked out before us.*
>
> — (HEBREWS 12:1 TPT)

Many of us desire a relationship with God or claim to be believers in Jesus, but forgiveness is a weakness that impacts our relationship with our Heavenly Father. Some of us withhold this aspect from God while allowing Him access to other parts of our lives. God wants to heal us from the inside out.

If you're reading this and feel ashamed of your mistakes, please remember that you don't have to be defined by them. Dwelling on your mistakes as regrets will only keep you stuck in every area, with additional consequences (Romans 8:1). Try to view each mistake as a lesson, write down the lessons learned, and accept the responsibility to improve. It's about progress, not perfection. The illusion of self-centered perfectionism undermines self-compassion.

This chapter is not for those who are defensive or unwilling to take responsibility for their actions. Yes, we can hold others accountable for their abuse, but who takes responsibility for our own reactions and actions?

First, I encourage you to humble yourself and confess your sins, receiving forgiveness through our Lord Jesus. Perhaps you feel like the offender and struggle to forgive yourself for your mistakes. Find reassurance in Jesus' redemption and love. You can start anew.

Meditate on the scriptures below:

New creation: II Corinthians 5:17
Acceptance: John 6:37
Righteousness: Romans 5:18–19
Repentance: Acts 3:19
Grace: Ephesians 2:8–9

THE GIFT OF FORGIVENESS

New life: Galatians 2:20 TPT
Nature of God: 1 John 1:8–10 MSG

Some may wonder if God still loves us after we have transgressed against Him. We cannot forget the nature of God, for doing so would diminish His divine essence. God is not human; He embodies love itself. He is neither our abuser nor someone who has neglected us. Some people hold God accountable for human mistakes, especially when wrongdoers claim to be His children. Others also blame God for the loss of a loved one or unfavorable outcomes.

Doing this hurts you by pushing you further away from the person who can truly make you whole and heal your pain. It's God who sees and understands your suffering the most.

God gave us His Son, Jesus, to die in our place so that we can believe in Him, experience intimacy with Him, and attain eternal life. God doesn't choose when He loves us; He respects our choices. He won't force us to love Him. If God could love us at our worst (Romans 5:7–8), what do you think about such love? His love does involve correction and discipline, which we often confuse with rejection.

God's love is unconditional and unending. We should find solace in this truth, especially when we make mistakes. He doesn't distance Himself from us, even when we feel He's far away. He wants us to run to Him for comfort, support, and reassurance. Instead, we often turn away in our filth, foolishness, pride, and stubbornness.

God alone possesses the power to redeem and save us. "It is because of the Lord's mercy and loving-kindness that we are not consumed, for His [tender] compassions do not fail. They are new every morning; great and abundant is Your stability and faithfulness" (Lamentations 3:22–23 AMPC).

Before Jesus, there was no hope on Earth or beyond this life. Jesus has brought us eternal hope beyond death. (Romans 5:10-11 AMPC)

Jesus' Nature

Offenses can either break us or strengthen us, depending on where we choose to direct our focus. When we seek God and grasp our purpose, offenses can serve as catalysts for personal growth and nurturing the fruit of the Spirit.

We often take offense too quickly when someone disagrees with us, forgetting that our differing views arise from our unique experiences and backgrounds. We should let love bring us together rather than allowing these differences to divide us. Sometimes, the most significant expression of love comes through honest rebuke when we are wrong (Proverbs 27:5). Being humble enough to listen can facilitate personal growth.

Extending forgiveness to ourselves and others is a vital expression of love. True love incorporates forgiveness, which requires adopting Jesus' humility (1 Corinthians 2:16).

Jesus exemplified forgiveness during His earthly ministry. He faced persecution and humiliation but still forgave those who wronged Him and interceded for our forgiveness (Luke 23:34, Hebrews 4:15–16).

CONSEQUENCES OF UNFORGIVENESS

Jesus warned us in the Bible that we would be offended: "Woe to the world because of offenses! For offenses must come, but woe to that man by whom the offense comes!" (Matthew 18:7). Here are some effects of unforgiveness:

Estranged Relationships and Hindered Prayers: Jesus taught us that forgiveness is essential. He encouraged us not only to offer forgiveness but also to seek it when others hold grievances against us. Holding onto unforgiveness can affect our relationships with others and God, leading to disobedience, whether we are the offender or the offended (Mark 11:25–26, Matthew 5:23–24), and can result in hindered prayer. "If I regard iniquity in my heart, the Lord will not hear" (Psalms 66:18). Unanswered prayers can mean we miss opportunities through others.

Access to Evil: Holding on to unforgiveness invites evil into every aspect of wellness, leading to various issues such as health problems (like high blood pressure and anxiety), financial struggles, substance dependence, and feelings of stagnation. The devil can exploit our unforgiveness and use it against us (II Corinthians 2:10–11).

Jesus buttressed this with the parable of the unforgiving servant in Matthew 18:21–35, which tells of a king who forgave a servant's debts of 10,000 talents (estimated to be

60 million denarii) out of compassion. Yet, this same servant had his debtor thrown in jail over 100 denarii.

Distraction and lack of productivity: Have you ever noticed how an offense can distract us, causing us to dwell on it for days and become unproductive? **The offense isn't just about the behavior that upset us; the action and our reaction often divert our attention from what truly deserves our focus, ultimately wasting precious time.**

Unforgiveness can distract us from our overall wellness. Financially, it can lead to excessive spending. Intellectually, it hampers our focus. Mentally, we may seek relief through substances. Socially, it often results in isolation, and spiritually, it strains our relationship with God and our ability to pray effectively.

If the purpose of an offense is not discerned, it will rob us of our potential for greatness and productivity. We cannot confront the impact of offenses on us without confronting the offense. Olajumoke Adenowo stated, "There is a choice between the offense and taking offense; you may offend me, but I choose not to be offended. Offense can rob you of your glory if people know what to say to offend you.

Unfruitfulness: Unforgiveness hinders us from experiencing the fullness of the Holy Spirit's fruit, causing us to become stagnant and potentially unappealing to others. When approached with humility, offenses can reveal our limitations and strengths. Our true essence, expressed through words and actions, reflects who we are (Proverbs 27:19). **Unhealed or poorly healed wounds cause a stench of**

negative thoughts, emotions, and unprofitable attitudes.

While we may have various gifts, many of us carry unhealed wounds that lead to negative thoughts and attitudes, limiting our potential. These emotional wounds often result in ineffective leadership across various areas, including organizations, marriages, and churches. John Bevere, an American evangelist, author, and co-founder of Messenger International, stated, "Many are unable to function properly in their calling because of the wounds and hurts that offenses have caused in their lives. They are hindered from fulfilling their full potential. Most often, it is a fellow believer who has hurt them."

Entitlement: Are you easily offended because you believe you deserve or have a right to certain privileges from people, situations, or God? Recognizing and accepting that no one owes you anything may alleviate this bitterness; otherwise, this mindset will continually limit you and your relationships. Unforgiveness hardens our hearts, preventing us from giving or receiving love without entitlement or manipulation.

In the Bible, Cain killed his brother Abel because he perceived permanent rejection from God and unresolved emotional pain. God disciplines those He loves. His rebuke of Cain and His gift were meant for repentance and good works, not as a function of permanent rejection. Sometimes, we confuse the two, leading to dire complications (Genesis 4:1–16).

Esau didn't confront his emotional pain from Jacob's deception, which led him to marry the wrong woman and grieve his parents (Genesis 26:34–35). Uncontrolled emotional pain can ruin even the best of circumstances due to selfishness.

Unnecessary war: Due to our bitterness, we may cause more trouble and poison the hearts of many, leading them astray (Hebrews 12:18 TPT).Nations have gone to war unnecessarily because of unforgiveness, leading to the loss of innocent lives. Traumatic losses can lead to unforgiveness in the survivor. Unforgiveness can, in turn, promote terrorism, generational differences, and future wars.

Generational pain: **Unforgiveness can be passed down from one generation to another, creating a cycle of chaos, bitterness, discord, and pain that spans generations.** Our actions don't always end with us. They can lead to a legacy of rejection and disaster, causing limited interdependent benefits and support opportunities.

BENEFITS OF FORGIVENESS

Forgiveness may be challenging, yet it is similar to generosity, both of which arise from God's love for us. We offer these as gifts to others, not as rewards for merit. When we express them genuinely, we mirror the essence of God and Jesus. Below are some benefits:

Physically
Forgiving others and oneself is linked to better physical health, reduced pain, improved immune function, and greater overall life satisfaction. It is also associated with healthier behaviors, fewer health symptoms, better cardiovascular

responses, lower blood pressure, and decreased mortality rates.[1]

Psychologically
Forgiveness enriches the soul, which affects other aspects of our lives (3 John 2 AMP).
Several randomized studies have demonstrated the benefits of forgiveness, which include improved sleep, lower levels of anxiety, depression, and hostility, reduced substance abuse, improved self-esteem, and increased life satisfaction.

Spiritually
God's love is unconditional; however, rewards are tied to obeying His commands, which include forgiving others. The gift of sonship grants access to all of God's blessings, including the forgiveness of sins (Matthew 6:12), greatness, the fruit of the Spirit (Galatians 5:22–23), prosperity in various areas, and generational blessings.

Generational Impact- Significance
Though he has passed away, Nelson Mandela is still celebrated for transforming his pain into purpose and power. Jesus was honored with the greatest name (Philippians 2:9-10) and granted the highest honor—sovereignty.

Are you struggling to forgive someone who has wronged, oppressed, and abused you but hasn't shown any remorse or apologized, leaving you feeling that no justice has been served? It's understandable to feel this way. However, it's not always our place to seek revenge. Even if we do have the power to take revenge, would we ever truly be satisfied? It's important to remember that there are consequences for the offender, as mentioned in Matthew 18:7 and Luke 17:1–4. Choosing to forgive and letting go of the desire for revenge can bring peace and healing to your life. I humbly express this, acknowledging that you may have faced terrible acts of cruelty directed at you or your loved ones.

Forgiveness is a complete mandate that God promises to reward, not when we forgive those with whom we hope to gain something in return, but when we forgive those with whom we may not wish to associate. You might think forgiveness was easy for Jesus since He is the Lord. The Bible contains several examples of individuals who demonstrated the same attitude as Jesus on Earth, including Joseph and Stephen. More recently, Corrie Ten Boom, a Holocaust survivor and author, also exemplified this attitude. She stated, 'I discovered that it is not on our forgiveness, any more than on our goodness, that the world's healing hinges, but on His." When He tells us to love our enemies, He gives along with the command, the love itself."

Now that you understand the importance of forgiveness toward God, others, and yourself. Let's examine another powerful tool that can aid you on your journey to healing: the power of gratitude.

CHAPTER ELEVEN

ATTITUDE OF GRATITUDE

Rejoice always...in everything give thanks; for this is the will of God in Christ Jesus for you.

— I THESSALONIANS 5:16,18

Doctor, "Why should I say thank you for what life owes me after all I have been through?" "Why do I take people and life for granted?" "Do I have a right to claim anything?" "How do I handle what I believe I deserve?"

What comes to mind when you think of gratitude? Do you think of it as much or little? Does it matter to you if you receive or give gratitude?

Gratitude is a powerful emotion that can profoundly impact our lives. According to Merriam-Webster, gratitude is the act of being appreciative of benefits received, whether it's the comfort that has been supplied or the discomfort that has been alleviated.

By cultivating gratitude daily, we can experience greater happiness, stronger relationships, and improved overall health. Expressing gratitude for the good things in our lives can transform us and our world. Gratitude requires an active process of acknowledging the goodness of others and those in your life.

Numerous scientific studies have shown that gratitude offers physical, psychological, and social benefits. Gratitude is a virtue that requires intentionality and provides significant benefits to individuals of all ages.

According to Drs. Fred Bryant and Joseph Veroff, psychology professors, there are three kinds of gratitude: reminiscence, savoring, and anticipation. Reminiscence is gratitude for what has already happened, savoring is gratitude for something happening in the present, and anticipation is gratitude for things you hope and expect to happen.

PSYCHOLOGICAL BENEFITS

Gratitude enhances well-being by promoting positive emotions, a positive affect, optimism, and a focus on positive psychology, ultimately leading to improved functioning.

Research has shown gratitude:

- Increases dopamine, a neurotransmitter associated

with motivation, attention, reward, and pleasure, motivating you to repeat behaviors such as gratitude
- Increases serotonin, the happy chemical that regulates our mood and well-being, and causes relaxation
- Activates the hippocampus and amygdala, thereby improving cognition and memory. When gratitude is expressed, activity in the medial prefrontal cortex associated with learning is increased

When we choose gratitude, the brain feels empowered, and feelings of hopelessness or helplessness are reduced. The brain cannot be thankful and worried at the same time; therefore, the more thankful one is, the less negative the person tends to be.

Negative experiences can lead to resentment and entitlement, which can be antidotes to gratitude. Personality flaws, such as narcissism and neuroticism, find gratitude challenging. Dr. Sonja Lyubomirsky, a psychologist, stated, "Gratitude is an antidote to negative emotions, a neutralizer of envy, hostility, worry, and irritation. It is savoring, not taking things for granted; it is present-oriented."

Gratitude has been described as the greatest of all virtues. However, focusing on positive experiences and expressing gratitude can be challenging because our brains are wired to recognize, reflect, and remember negative experiences as survival mechanisms, increasing the risk of depression, burnout, anxiety, and other mental disorders.

Gratitude has been studied as a personality trait and an emotional state. As a personality trait, gratitude refers to a person's natural tendency to recognize and express gratitude without needing specific events or experiences. In contrast, as an emotional state, gratitude arises from a desire to reciprocate when one feels they have received a positive outcome.

Several studies have shown a connection between trait gratitude and intense emotional experiences of gratitude. While emotional state gratitude is a temporary psychological experience, trait gratitude is a lasting disposition. Trait gratitude has been shown to increase prosocial behaviors, including empathy, forgiveness, and willingness to help others.[2] The practice of state gratitude through daily and weekly journaling has been shown to improve overall well-being, including fewer health complaints and a positive outlook toward life.[4]

Gratitude reduces frustration and resentment over the possessions and achievements of others. You cannot be full of appreciation and envy at the same time. Regret is a form of dwelling on the negative; it's a counterfactual emotion produced by perceptions of what might have been, which leads to anxiety, unhappiness, and depression.[1]

Gratitude improves self-esteem and decreases materialism. It makes personal success less likely to be defined using material accomplishments and possessions.[2] No wonder Albert Einstein stated, "There are only two ways to live your life.

One is as though nothing is a miracle. The other is as though everything is a miracle."

Dr Alex Wood, a psychology professor, and his team found that:

- Grateful individuals tend to interpret situations more positively due to their thought patterns
- They are more likely to make constructive coping assessments and are less prone to deny problems.
- Gratitude fosters positive emotions that can help protect against mental health disorders and promote overall well-being.
- Gratitude also broadens thought and action options, helping individuals build resources for long-term well-being.[3]

PHYSICAL BENEFITS

Gratitude improves physical health because:

- It decreases bodily complaints
- It promotes exercise
- It improves sleep (Gratitude regulates deep and restful sleep by activating the hypothalamus.)
- It increases parasympathetic activity, which controls physiological efficiency that reduces stress, heart rate, and hypertension

Gratitude helps reduce cortisol release and enhances the body's immune function. This thereby improves well-being (e.g., life satisfaction, happiness, and positive affect), physical health (e.g., blood pressure, glycemic control, and inflammatory markers), and mental health (e.g., reducing depression and anxiety). Gratitude has been shown to reduce subjective feelings of pain. When patients in pain thought of gratitude, they experienced less pain by regulating the level of dopamine.[4]

SOCIAL BENEFITS

Gratitude leads to:

- Greater gratitude
- Life satisfaction
- Optimism
- Prosocial behavior, which strengthens relationships

Gratitude enhances communication, fosters empathy, and strengthens interpersonal relationships. Studies show that gratitude activates the ventromedial prefrontal cortex (VMPFC), which is associated with pure altruism, the desire to give and be good to others. Expressing gratitude benefits individuals and society.[5]

Research indicates that feeling grateful at work is associated with enhanced well-being, mental health, and job-related outcomes. Gratitude correlates with positive emotions, life, and job satisfaction, reduced depressive

ATTITUDE OF GRATITUDE

symptoms, and improved job performance and commitment behavior.[6]

Healthcare providers who practiced "Three Good Things" for two weeks experienced reduced burnout and depressive symptoms, along with improved work-life integration and increased happiness, which persisted for a year. Expressing gratitude is crucial for these benefits and may help emotionally healthy individuals and others.[7]

Melody Beattle, an American author, stated:

> *Gratitude makes sense of our past, brings peace for today, and creates a vision for tomorrow. Gratitude unlocks the fullness of life. It turns what we have into enough and more. It turns denial into acceptance, chaos into order, and confusion into clarity. It can turn a meal into a feast, a house into a home, a stranger into a friend.*

SPIRITUAL BENEFITS

Practicing gratitude:

- Softens our hearts in humility
- Brings contentment (I Timothy 6:6)
- Focuses our trust in God
- Renews hope
- Brings multiplication and increase (Psalm 67:5–7, Jeremiah 30:19)
- Leads to joy, a fruit of the Holy Spirit (Galatians 5:22)

Joy

Joy is not dependent on emotion or situation but on contentment in knowing God's character and power. Joy can be contagious and energizing, but depression can be contagious and deplete our energy. Joy has a healing effect, like medicine, while a broken spirit can cause you to feel weak and hopeless (Proverbs 17:22). We can exchange our depression and anxiety for the joy of the Lord, which changes us for the better and renews our hope (James 1:2-4).

Joy and appreciating God for who He is will unlock additional blessings, including a positive change in attitude and our outlook on life. With joy, we draw and receive blessings from the spiritual realms (Isaiah 12:3). ***Rejoicing is a powerful remedy for emotional and mental health challenges***.

The state of the heart

Giving thanks is a heart process. Thanksgiving flows from a heart full of gratitude, not worries, complaints, or focus on what has not yet been done. Sometimes, our broken hearts need a deep cleansing of the debris from unhealed wounds. Maybe a spiritual heart transplant is required for our broken and hardened hearts caused by multiple damages and scars (Ezekiel 36:26).

A hardened heart can give false control over bitterness and the risk of vulnerability, preventing us from experiencing positive emotions such as love, joy, and peace.

EXPRESSION OF GRATITUDE

Gratitude is a mindset. It's a perspective that can attract additional things for which to be grateful. A bitter heart attracts more disaster.

If you're from North America, you may be familiar with the annual holiday, which takes place on the fourth Thursday of November, involving thanksgiving through feasting. President Abraham Lincoln established it as a national holiday during the Civil War. Other countries, such as the Netherlands, Canada, Grenada, Saint Lucia, Liberia, Australia, Germany, China, United Kingdom, Japan, and unofficially, Brazil and the Philippines, also celebrate Thanksgiving.

Many Nigerian churches worldwide hold thanksgiving services on a specific Sunday each month.

While those are great reminders to pause and reflect on the blessings one has received, practicing gratitude should be done daily due to its numerous benefits. Gratitude can be expressed verbally or nonverbally in simple or elaborate ways. What's important is that it's thoughtful.

Like any behavior, gratitude can be cultivated by practice.

Gratitude involves being mindful of the blessings in one's life. We must guard our hearts against anything that distracts us from acknowledging our blessings and the blessers. *You cannot be thankful if you're not thoughtful*. A famous Yoruba proverb in Nigeria states, *Ẹni ti ó bá mọ inú rò, á mọ ọpẹ́ dá*. It means, "Whoever can think, reflect, or reason will know how to give thanks." Giving thanks should not be limited to a seasonal practice; it should be a daily habit.

Unfortunately, distractions such as bitterness can diminish the ability to appreciate any goodness done to us by others.

A bitter heart cannot truly cherish or enjoy anything good, as all experiences are viewed through a negative mindset. Gratitude and bitterness are personality traits that significantly contribute to the outcome of our lives, either positively or negatively.

Gratitude is not rooted in perfection but in appreciation for the progress made and, if possible, for what remains to be done. Most people still wait for all things to be perfect before showing gratitude.

If you can appreciate what you have, starting with the ability to read this book, then you can handle more. Whatever blessings you appreciate will magnify, while those you disregard will depreciate.

The giver and receiver of gratitude benefit from it; however, the giver may gain even more.

Expressing gratitude to our helpers and supporters strengthens our relationships. Imagine how you feel when someone appreciates, values, or loves you, especially without anything in return.

Gratitude in our relationships can open doors of networking, greatness, connections, and recommendations.

ATTITUDE OF GRATITUDE

The two great commandments emphasize our love for God and how we treat others. God values relationships and loves people. He created us to be interdependent with one another. The goal is not to worship humans but to honor everyone, as you never know who might play a role in your greatness.

You become whatever has your focus.

If you focus on the negativity in your life and the world, you will likely become negative. If you focus on the good you have, no matter how little, you may experience more positivity. You can see the glass half empty or half full or be grateful that there is a glass in the first place. It all depends on your perspective.

Attentional bias refers to the tendency to focus selectively on a particular aspect while neglecting others. This bias can significantly influence our perceptions and decision-making processes, potentially contributing to the development of anxiety and depression. Studies have shown that individuals with anxiety and depression tend to exhibit a more significant bias toward negative stimuli.[8]

Gratitude shifts our mindset from worrying to rest and contentment, thereby reducing panic from a place of fearful anticipation, competition, and comparison. Gratitude shifts our focus from scarcity to fullness. Suddenly, what seemed out of control becomes within our control because we intentionally chose thanksgiving.

Ingratitude

According to Merriam-Webster's definition, ingratitude is "forgetfulness of or poor return for kindness received." "It is the lack of awareness or consideration of the possible worse outcome of your past, present, and future."

Sometimes, imagining a worse outcome than our current situation can help us appreciate what we have and be grateful for things that others may desire, including things we may not value as much.

Ingratitude can lead to an attitude of entitlement, or vice versa, resulting in resentment, envy, jealousy, comparison, and competition, among other adverse effects. Often, ingratitude is rooted in pride, self-sufficiency, or a bitter attitude.

People who don't express gratitude may struggle to see good in themselves. Ingratitude can stem from a lack of empathy or compassion toward oneself or others. Max Lucado, an American author and Minister at Oak Hills Church, stated, "The devil doesn't have to steal anything from you; all he has to do is make you take it for granted."

Complaining

It's essential to express our emotions for our mental well-being, but complaining can hurt our mental health if it's done ineffectively or unproductively. Complaining involves expressing displeasure, dissatisfaction, or resentment, often by blaming someone or something. Dr. Robin Kowalski, a psychology professor, stated, "There are two types of complaining: expressive complaining, which is venting, and instrumental complaining, which is designed to accomplish a specific outcome."

Complaining isn't always bad, but its outcome largely depends on how it's done. Before complaining, it's essential to consider the timing, tone, attitude, and desired outcome to ensure an effective and productive complaint. Venting is the release of built-up negativity, often focused on seeking attention and validation while ignoring proposed solutions.

Complaining to the same person frequently or about everything can lead to a negative outlook. Constant negativity can lead to increased stress levels, anxiety, and depression. Like most stressful activities, complaining can shrink the hippocampus, which affects memory, emotions, and learning. When we complain without a strategy, we focus on the negative aspects of a situation and overlook any positive aspects.

Persistent complaining affects both the person complaining and those listening to the negativity. Complaining can decrease overall happiness and lead to a negative outlook on life. Complaining can be contagious. When we complain, we often seek validation from others, resulting in a cycle of negativity and complaining. This can damage relationships and lead to feelings of isolation and loneliness.

Unproductive complaining is costly in terms of physical, emotional, social, and spiritual consequences. While God loves it when we share our anguish and feelings with Him, complaining that focuses on blaming Him and is devoid of our reverence for His might and power displeases Him and can strain our relationship with Him (Numbers 11). It is healthy to respectfully share our emotions and frustrations with God and supportive people who can listen and offer solutions.

Focusing on identifying a solution to the problem, practicing gratitude, and emphasizing the positive aspects can benefit mental health. It can help reduce overall stress levels and increase contentment and happiness.

A seeming disappointment may feel like an unanswered prayer, leading us to complain, but it may be a redirection to something good—a blessing. This was my experience during the process of applying for US residency. US residency application can be overwhelming, especially for international medical graduates like me. Despite meeting all the requirements, the process can be quite nerve-wracking. I was thrilled to receive numerous interview offers when applying for psychiatry positions. However, my excitement was short-lived when I didn't match with my top-choice position.

I experienced a range of emotions, from grumbling and crying to questioning why things didn't go my way despite fervent prayers and fasting. I turned to scriptures and music that persistently reminded me of the consciousness of God's presence and that all is working out for my good (Romans 8:28). This shift in perspective helped me move from a place of entitlement to one of gratitude, especially for being given a spot in the first place.

Even though I didn't fully understand the situation, I trusted the process. And guess what? As I figured out how to settle in a new state, I discovered that my extended family was already living there. This unexpected turn of events led to a beautiful period of growth and connection, encompassing the church community, clinical experiences, and a network of supportive colleagues. I remain grateful to God and the people for the enriching experiences and the valuable lessons learned during that time.

Self-assessment of gratitude

Please see the questionnaires and write your answers in your workbook. Now that you know the importance of a grateful attitude, read the next chapter to discover how music can be a helpful tool.

CHAPTER TWELVE

MUSICAL DELIGHT

So then faith comes by hearing and hearing by the word of God.

— ROMANS 10:17

Doctor, "Why should I care about the music I listen to?" What's the big deal about music? Can't I sing or listen to any music I like?"

Music is a powerful expression that transcends language barriers and unites people. According to the Merriam-Webster Dictionary, it's not just a collection of sounds but a beautiful combination of melody, rhythm, and harmony that voices, instruments, or machines can produce.

Music has the power to move us, inspire us, and even heal us. Music can touch our souls and lift our spirits, whether it's a soothing melody or an energizing beat.

A music genre is an artistic, musical, or literary composition category characterized by a particular style, form, or content. Some music genres include gospel, rock, pop, funk, country, soul, Latin, reggae, electronic, hip-hop, punk rock, blues, jazz, R&B, and many more.

Whether you're a musician or not a music lover, you should always consider immersing yourself in music and experiencing its magic. Albert Einstein stated, "If I were not a physicist, I would probably be a musician. I often think in music. I live my daydreams in music. I see my life in terms of music."

Listening to music, whether the lyrics or the melody, can create an earworm—a catchy tune that lingers in your mind and influences your thoughts, emotions, and actions. This influence can even extend to your waking moments. For instance, after repeatedly hearing the children's song "Baby Shark" for my kids, it became an earworm for me, often playing in my mind throughout my daily activities.

We should be intentional about our music choices. Our subconscious mind stores music to be recalled later, much like it does with other experiences.

We frequently turn to music that resonates with our current emotions, but sometimes, this choice can be unhelpful or counterproductive. It's essential to be aware of how the music we listen to affects our mood and productivity.

THE SCIENCE OF MUSIC

Music originates as sound waves that stimulate our auditory cortices and other brain areas, including those responsible for memory, rhythm, movement, and emotional processing.

The brain regulates physiological and cognitive processes, with connections in the nervous system allowing each to influence the other. Music can significantly impact our experiences with people, places, and things through our senses.

Neuroimaging studies have demonstrated that music activates brain circuits associated with essential survival rewards, including food and money. It specifically stimulates the nucleus accumbens, a key area associated with dopamine release and addiction.

Music is powerful on the brain and our bodies. According to Dr David Silbersweig, one of the pioneers of functional neuroimaging research in psychiatry:

> *"Music causes structural and functional changes in the brain, both after immediate exposure and over weeks, months, and years later. These changes can promote emotional healing by activating certain areas of the brain involved in emotional processing, abstract thinking, attention, reward, and motivation. If these changes persist over some time, they create new neuronal pathways that will compensate for the disrupted signals in the brain."*[1]

Brain activation patterns also vary based on whether we listen to music, perform rehearsed pieces, or improvise new ones, music.[2]

Music and language

Neuroscience has revealed that music helps with language as they share overlapping brain networks.

Babies understand language as they respond to the rhythm and melody of a language before they understand the meaning. Musically trained children have better reading comprehension skills.[3]

Plato, an Ancient Greek Philosopher, stated, "I would teach children music, physics, and philosophy, but most importantly music, for the patterns in music and all the arts are the keys to learning."

Physical benefits of music

As stated in prior chapters, when stressed, the body releases inflammatory markers and stimulates the adrenal gland to release cortisol. Music releases endorphins, which help with relaxation. It also relieves stress by affecting the ANS, including parasympathetic and heart rate variability.

Classical music has been shown to have a positive effect on heart rate, blood pressure, and mood states.[4]

Psychological benefits

Music has been shown to affect our thoughts, feelings, and actions. Therefore, it should not be surprising that musical therapy fosters wellness. When we hear a tune, we become overwhelmed with strong emotions.

Music therapy uses the power of music to address physical, emotional, cognitive, and social needs within a therapeutic relationship. Sessions may involve listening to music, engaging in musical improvisation or composition, and exploring related emotions and thoughts, guided by a trained therapist who uses evidence-based techniques.

Music activates regions within the central nervous system (CNS) that are also responsive to oxytocin—the hormone associated with bonding, social connection, attachment, social memory, emotional empathy, trust, generosity, and the suppression of anxiety.

Music was found to be beneficial during the COVID-19 pandemic crisis. A study involving over 5,600 people from 11 countries found that music played a significant role in helping individuals cope during lockdown and achieve their well-being goals across cultural, age, and gender lines.[5]

Music has been shown in multiple studies to have several benefits, including:

- Enjoyment
- Venting negative emotions

- Pain management
- Reduced anxiety
- Reduced depression
- Reduced stress
- Improved sleep
- Elevated mood
- Motivation
- Confidence
- Cognition
- Memory

An overview of 349 studies on mental disorders, such as schizophrenia, bipolar disorder, and major depression, found that 68.5% of music-based interventions had positive results.[6]

Music helps with awareness, self-acceptance, and relaxation. Thus, it has been studied to promote eating habits, reduce emotional exhaustion, and improve stress-related disorders.

Music interventions have shown positive effects on the behavior and cognition of individuals with Alzheimer's, improving quality of life, mainly when implemented in the form of individualized playlists for relaxation.

Oliver Sacks, a British neurologist and writer, stated:

> *Music can move us to the heights or depths of emotion. It can persuade us to buy something or remind us of our first date. It can lift us out of depression when nothing else can. It can get us dancing to*

its beat. *But the power of music goes much, much further. Indeed, music occupies more areas of our brain than language does—humans are a musical species.*

Music and dancing

Science has revealed that our bodies are naturally wired to respond to the beat of music and can't resist moving to the rhythm. Dancing is a fun and enjoyable way to exercise both the body and mind. Engaging in music and dancing can improve mental health.

Dancing to your favorite tunes is a great way to get your heart pumping and improve your physical and mental well-being while having a good time. It can make you feel happier and more energized, keeping your mind and body in shape.

Spiritual benefits

The frequency of listening to religious music has been shown to be associated with:

- A decrease in death anxiety[7]
- An increase in life satisfaction and self-esteem
- A sense of control among older U.S. adults

The Impact of Music on Children

Music has been shown in several studies to reduce anxiety, pain, and depression, including before and during medical procedures.[8]

Music plays a vital role in the socialization of children and adolescents. Music provides entertainment and serves as a distraction from problems. It's a way to relieve tension and boredom, deal with loneliness, manage emotional states or moods, and establish relationships in diverse settings.

Some individuals use music in their identity formation, with their music preferences providing a sense of group identity within youth culture.[9] Their music preference may reflect their development's internal conflict and turmoil.

Lyrics and the genre of music

Different parts of the brain are activated depending on the type of music, whether the music involves consonant or dissonant elements, is syntonic or not, contains variations in temporal dynamics, or evokes an emotional response or memory.[10]

There have been several concerns related to the lyrics of some genres of music and their impact on children and adolescents, as lyrics have become more explicit in their references to drugs, sex, and violence over the years.

The preference for certain types of music has been studied to be associated with risky behaviors, such as the association of "rave" music or electronic music dance events with drug and alcohol use.[11] Heavy metal and some rock music have been associated with an increased risk of suicide.[12]

However, people's self-reports of negative feelings or emotions when listening to music are the best predictors of the risk in adolescents related to music. A correlation exists between the negative emotional response to music and risk-taking behavior in children and adolescents.[13]

Fans of heavy metal music reported:

- More problems with school authorities and teachers and, in some cases, conduct disorders[14]
- Depression
- Delinquency risk behaviors[13]
- Smoking
- Below average performance and academic problems in elementary school [11]

Exposure to violence, sexual messages, sexual stereotypes, and the use of substances of abuse in music videos may produce significant changes in the behaviors and attitudes of young viewers, therefore encouraging the analysis of content in music videos.[15]

Some have argued that misogynistic behaviors may not be related to music/lyrics alone but to socio-cultural norms and personality tendencies.

American Academy of Pediatrics stated, "The preference for heavy-metal music, rap, and associated genres among adolescents must alert us to an increased vulnerability and tendency toward risky behaviors."[15]

The impact of lyrics and genre doesn't affect the young only, as more negative stereotype attitudes/aggression have been observed in men with a preference for heavy-metal and rap toward women[16]. **If music can improve our thoughts, feelings, and actions, then it can certainly have the opposite effect.**

Music and personality traits

We engage in music by listening, producing, or singing. Music helps us connect with others, ourselves, and the spiritual realm. Music reveals who we are, including our personality traits, experiences, preferences, and choices.

Some have discovered a "Big Five" set of musical preferences:[17]

1. Sophisticated: These sounds are instrumental, complex, inspiring, intelligent, and characterized by classical or marching bands. They tend to be high on Openness to experience.
2. Unpretentious: These sounds are characterized by a relaxing, romantic, and melancholic tone, often associated with country music. They tend to score high on Agreeableness and Conscientiousness and exhibit a slight tendency towards Extraversion.

3. Intense: Distorted, electric, fast, loud, and aggressive sounds are appreciated, such as those found in punk rock and heavy metal. There is a tendency to be high on openness to Experience and least conscientious.
4. Mellow: Very relaxing and romantic sounds, sometimes sad and characterized by R&B, soul, and soft rock. There is a tendency to be high on Openness to Experience.
5. Contemporary: Electric sounds dominate various genres, from rap to electronica. There is a slight tendency to be high on Extraversion and Agreeableness.

THE BIBLE AND MUSIC

The Bible emphasizes the power of music, which has been a vital part of God's adoration since the beginning of time. God sings (Zephaniah 3:17), and He made all living things, including trees, mountains (Isaiah 49:13), human beings, and animals, with the ability to sing and make music. Bach, a German composer, stated, "I play the notes as they are written, but it is God who makes the music."

> Let the heavens rejoice, let the earth be glad; let them say among the nations, "The Lord reigns!" Let the sea resound, and all that is in it; let the fields be jubilant, and everything in them! Let the trees of the forest sing, let them sing for joy before the Lord.
>
> — (I CHRONICLES 16:31–33)

Louie Giglio, an author and lead pastor of Passion City Church in America, showcased a mash-up of stars and whales singing to God. He stated that some of the big ones among the billion stars include the Sun, Betelgeuse, Hubble sees, Canis Majoris, Sirius, Pollux, Arcturus, Rigel, Antares, Mu Cephei, W Cephei, etc.

Even the devil was created as a beautiful archangel and anointed cherub with music as the core of his being. He now propagates music to defy God's will (Ezekiel 28:12–15).

Positive uses of music as seen in the Bible:

As a weapon of war
In the Biblical story of King Jehoshaphat and the Israelites, amid music, God brought victory to the Israelites over their enemies (2 Chron. 20:22–24).
Another case is seen with Joshua and the wall of Jericho, which collapsed at the sound of trumpets and loud shouts, as described in Joshua 6.

> *When the priests sounded the trumpet blast, Joshua commanded the army, "Shout! For the Lord has given you the city!" When the trumpets sounded, the army shouted, and at the sound of the trumpet, when the men gave a loud shout, the wall collapsed, so everyone charged straight in, and they took the city.*
>
> — (JOSHUA 6:16, 20)

To exalt God

When God parted the Red Sea and delivered the Israelites from the Egyptians, Moses, Miriam, and the children of Israel sang to the Lord and spoke, saying: "I will sing to the Lord, For He has triumphed gloriously! The horse and its rider He has thrown into the sea!" (Exodus 15:1).

God desires for us to come into His presence with singing and magnifying His name. (Psalms 100:1–2). Praising the Lord looks lovely on the lips of God's people. It is good to praise the Lord.

To inspire and appreciate others

Music can inspire and motivate individuals to pursue their goals. It also is a powerful tool for expressing appreciation and admiration for others. The Bible shows an example of this practice through the women who sang and danced to honor and celebrate the victories of David and King Saul over the Philistines (1 Samuel 18:6–7).

In the United States and around the globe, music plays a significant role in various settings, including cheerleading, halftime shows, and marching bands. In Nigeria, there is no exception; music is deeply embedded in our culture and is essential in many aspects of life. It is often used during special events to encourage people to donate to causes or during performances by musical bands. During my time in Nigeria in secondary/high school, specific songs were sung to motivate athletes toward success. Music is a remarkable tool for conveying messages of value, appreciation, and motivation with a profoundly positive psychological impact.

To change our mood and the atmosphere of an environment
Music has the power to influence our moods and emotions in both positive and negative ways. One positive example of music therapy is found in the story of King Saul, who experienced relief from his torment when David played the harp for him (1 Samuel 16:23).
On the other hand, music can also hurt our mood. This is illustrated by King Saul's anger, provoked by the lyrics and songs sung by women celebrating David's victory over the Philistines. King Saul had felt that David was more highly praised than he was. (1 Samuel 18:5-9).

Have you ever felt a certain way and noticed that music either worsened your mood or transformed it into something completely different? I have experienced both. Listening to music about God's faithfulness has often softened my heart or energized me, changing my atmosphere when I was feeling frustrated or down. As I mentioned in Chapter 10, listening to music that speaks of God's unconditional love and reading Scripture transformed my mood from feeling low to one of gratitude. **Music can soften or harden the heart, influencing whether we seek to please ourselves or honor God.**

To interact with the spiritual realms
Music is not only a cultural and therapeutic tool but also a means to connect with the spiritual realm. It serves as a conduit for spiritual activities on earth; as Ludwig Beethoven, a German composer and pianist, once acknowledged, "Music is the mediator between the spiritual and the sensual

life." When a musician played, Prophet Elisha was able to prophesy the mind of God, and the prophecy came to pass as declared (2 Kings 3:15–17).

When Paul and Silas were jailed in the New Testament, they sang and prayed. The power of God broke their chains (Acts 16:25–26).

For encouragement, connection, and communication with one another Hans Christian Anderson, a Danish writer and poet, stated, "Where words fail, music speaks." We must follow the Bible's guidance and actively encourage one another with spiritual songs. The strength and inspiration we gain from the power of music can help us navigate life's challenges. Therefore, let us be resolute and committed to uplifting each other with the soulful melodies of spiritual songs (Ephesians 5:18–20).

Music has the power to either strengthen our faith or fuel our fear. The choice is ours.

Now that you understand the impact of your playlist on your mood let's explore other ways to care for yourself.

CHAPTER THIRTEEN

NURTURE YOU

It's useless to rise early and go to bed late and work your worried fingers to the bone.

Don't you know he enjoys giving rest to those he loves?

— PSALMS 127:2 TPT

"Doctor, why do I always try to keep going without taking a rest?" I prioritize everything and everyone above myself. Why do I feel bad about making some time for myself? Is self-care not selfish?"

Self-care is necessary because it's easy to feel drained by multiple responsibilities. Failing to make time to replenish, reset, rejuvenate, and repair can become destructive. The lack of healthy stress management can increase the risk of impairments in the eight pillars of wellness: mental, relational, spiritual, physical, financial, occupational, environmental, and intellectual.

SCIENCE OF SELF-CARE

As stated throughout this book, stress releases cortisol, the hormone that activates the fight-or-flight response for survival. Coping mechanisms should be targeted at increasing the brain's release of these hormones:

- Dopamine (reward with excitement)
- Serotonin (feel good)
- Oxytocin (bonding with others)
- Endorphins (provide healthy safety, survival, and recovery and decrease the risk of burnout)

You cannot be a good spouse, parent, friend, professional, child, or anything else to someone else without first being good to yourself. You cannot give what you don't have.

You must first secure yourself before you can help others up a cliff. We should fill our cups first; we can't pour from an empty cup. You must love yourself first if you want to love others properly. This fundamental principle enables you to extend love to others (Mark 12:31).

Our intentions become purified when we learn to please God while caring for ourselves. We transform from self-centeredness to God-centeredness. This shift empowers us to receive and give God's love, enabling us to treat others with kindness, patience, and understanding.

Is your love for others God-pleasing or self-absorbing? Is it focused on manipulating others from a sense of entitlement? Is it out of humility or pride?

Self-care involves looking after yourself.

Self-care is not:

- Being full of yourself or thinking of yourself all the time, which is selfishness
- Making the world about you
- Intended to end with you
- Self-absorbing or self-seeking
- Manipulating others out of entitlement
- Only about external care to cope with internal stress

Self-care is:

- Prioritizing God's love and self-love over being loved by others
- Providing vital requirements to oneself for sustenance and well-being in every area
- Any healthy activity with the end goal of enhancing productivity and reaching others
- In the quality and not solely in quantity
- Involves regulation of the nervous system
- Involves both internal and external care, but more internal practices to cope with internal stress
- Extending compassion and kindness to oneself

Airplane

An airplane experiences a drop in atmospheric oxygen level as it ascends. Humans require approximately 100 mmHg of oxygen pressure to maintain adequate blood oxygen saturation levels and prevent oxygen loss (hypoxia), which can cause multiple bodily damages, including confusion, lightheadedness, and loss of consciousness. Above 12,500 feet of altitude, the atmospheric oxygen level drops below 100 mmHg.

According to the Federal Aviation Administration (FAA), whenever there is a drop in cabin pressure, oxygen masks are deployed to provide at least 10 to 14 minutes of oxygen at a pressure of at least 122 mmHg. This gives the pilot sufficient time to descend to a level of 10,000 feet or lower. After you board, before the plane takes off, you will hear the flight attendant instruct you to put on your oxygen mask first before assisting others. You're advised to wear yours first before helping others, as you only have 30 seconds to put on your oxygen mask. **You can only be of help to others when you're alive.**

Similarly, we must prioritize nurturing ourselves for self-enrichment and empowerment before extending this to others. If we don't, it may harm our survival and health. This becomes more critical as we become busier, such as when the airplane ascends to a higher altitude.

Nurture

Merriam-Webster defines nurture as "to supply nourishment."

Nourishment is "the food or other substances necessary for growth, health, and good condition." Therefore, nurturing yourself involves providing food and other substances needed for growth and well-being. Ignoring nurturing can lead to stagnation, decline, failure, unhealthiness, and other detrimental conditions.

The goal of nourishment is to regain or maintain wellness in all aspects of life. Nurturing is effective when you recognize the timing and type of enrichment that is necessary. Depending on the nature of the enrichment, cultivating may require varying levels of activity.

Categories and examples of nourishment include:

- Physical nourishment: This encompasses a range of essential elements, including food, water, rest, sunlight, exercise, bathing, sleep, illness prevention, and sexual health, among others.
- Mental nourishment: This encompasses self-compassion, giving and receiving hugs, therapeutic crying, appropriate laughter, singing, respecting humor, advocating for yourself, contentment, kind words, vacations, rest, engaging in hobbies, and taking breaks from social media, among other things.
- Spiritual nourishment: This consists of prayer, meditating on God's Word, contemplative reflection, retreats, rest, and fasting.
- Financial nourishment: This involves spending within

your means, financial planning, analysis, and both short—and long-term investments.
- Environmental nourishment: This encompasses healthy exposure to sunlight, wind, food, and chemicals, as well as having a comfortable couch and bed to relax, along with other elements that make your environment conducive to overall well-being.
- Social nourishment: This involves striking a balance between personal and social time, establishing healthy boundaries, and intentionally investing in growth-oriented relationships rather than those that drain your energy. In any relationship, you're either giving or receiving value.
- Intellectual nourishment: This includes critical thinking, learning multiple methods for accomplishing tasks, mastering time management, and developing your ideas.
- Occupational nourishment: This entails striking a balance between work and leisure, ensuring that your career path aligns with your goals and success, and performing an individual SWOT analysis.

Nurturing yourself involves engaging in healthy activities that recharge, repair, and rejuvenate you, ultimately leading to greater productivity.

Repairing is a powerful method to restore something that is broken or impaired. Recharging effectively replenishes your energy and spirit. By rejuvenating yourself, you bring new vigor to every aspect of your life. These elements are key to unlocking your full potential, equipping you to face any challenges with confidence and determination. A deficiency in self-care can lead to breakdowns, wear and tear, exhaustion, and, ultimately, destruction.

Warning signs you need self-nurture/self-care:

- Feeling quickly tired, exhausted, or depleted
- Easily irritable or angered
- Unusual criticism of yourself or others
- Withdrawing from the world or feeling emotionally numb
- Avoiding pleasurable activities
- Poor concentration
- Unusual deviation in your thoughts, feelings and behavior
- Difficulty making decisions in the eight pillars of wellness
- Constantly feeling guilty or overwhelmed
- Consistently working too hard or too long hours
- Multiple health problems
- Prayerlessness
- Unusual selfishness

Rest

Rest is the essential nourishment for all aspects of wellness. It should not be seen as giving up but rather as a thoughtful pause characterized by reduced activity across the eight dimensions. When we neglect rest, we invite exhaustion and burnout into every facet of our lives. The key is to maintain a proper balance; an imbalance between rest and metabolic activities can have harmful effects.

You may take pride in being able to function without adequate rest, but this mindset can be detrimental. Rest represents a form of self-care that resonates across all dimensions of wellness.

Many people equate sleep with rest, but they are not the same thing. It's entirely possible to sleep and still feel unrested if your mind doesn't find the necessary quiet.

Our Almighty God, as powerful as He is, modeled rest during the creation:

> *"And on the seventh day, God completed His work, and He rested on the seventh day from all His work." Then God blessed the seventh day and sanctified it because He rested from all His work that He had created and made.*
>
> — (GENESIS 2:2–3)

> "Rest" here does not imply that God slept. God neither sleeps nor slumbers
>
> — (PSALMS 121:4).

Rest is not a luxury; it is a necessity. Jesus showed us its significance, so we must take a cue from Him and prioritize it in our lives. What use are we to others or ourselves when we are worn out?

> *The apostles then rendezvoused with Jesus and reported on all that they had done and taught. Jesus said, "Come by yourselves; let's take a break and get some rest." For there was constant coming and going. They didn't even have time to eat.*
>
> — (MARK 6:31–32 MSG)

Factors that influence rest:

Sleep
Sleep is essential for achieving rest, and a lack of sleep affects productivity and effectiveness.

According to the CDC:

> *A third of adults in the United States report that they get less than the recommended amount of sleep each night. Not getting enough sleep is linked with many chronic diseases and conditions, such as type 2 diabetes, heart disease, obesity, and depression, that threaten our nation's health. Not getting enough sleep can lead to motor vehicle crashes and mistakes at work, which cause a lot of injury and disability each year. An average adult between ages eighteen and sixty requires seven hours or more of sleep; the amount of sleep we need changes as we age.*

You may need more or less sleep than the average person—perhaps six or ten hours is sufficient for you. This doesn't mean you're abnormal; what matters is getting enough restorative sleep. It's not a competition; instead, we should focus on the hours our bodies need to achieve adequate repair during sleep.

Our bodies repair, and our brains declutter during sleep, much like a laptop needs proper shutdown and reboot. Prioritize restorative sleep, as research indicates that insufficient sleep can lead to emotional distress and impaired emotional awareness in others and ourselves.

Fear and worry can disrupt sleep. The Bible reminds us: "For You have delivered my soul from death... that I may walk before God in the light of the living" (Psalms 56:13). True rest comes from trusting God, who sustains and protects us. Rest cannot be bought; it comes from the profound revelation of knowledge of God.

Unrest does not come from God; He desires to grant rest to those He loves. **While there are medications that can induce sleep, none can guarantee that you will wake up to life.** Only God can provide peace and security (Psalms 4:8, Psalm 127:1).

Is your sleep affected by worrying about not getting adequate sleep? Do you struggle with closing your eyes at night due to fear of dying? This is a common cause of anxiety.

Anxiety
Anxiety and worry are obstacles to relaxation, often arising from fear or feelings of insufficiency and inadequacy. While being concerned is natural, persistent worry can lead to restlessness and impaired decision-making. Anxiety becomes a disorder when it hinders daily functioning. That's why God tells us not to worry, as He meets our daily needs (Matthew 6:25–34, 6:11).

Contentment
Contentment is a state of being satisfied, and true rest comes from finding contentment in something or someone. Are you God-made or self-made? Comparing your experiences and struggles to those of others can stem from emotional pain, ultimately leading to a deeper understanding of yourself and self-discovery. However, unhealed pain often breeds comparison and competition.

In the Bible, Job focused on his growth rather than comparing himself to others, reminding us that our journeys are unique and not meant for comparison. Contentment is an antidote to comparison. Finding contentment in God is especially beneficial (1 Timothy 6:6). If you are self-made, you may feel overwhelmed, as you will always experience some lack. Our true sufficiency comes from God (2 Corinthians 3:5).

Authenticity
According to Merriam-Webster, authenticity is "made or done in the same way as an original; not false or imitation."

Lacking authenticity can disrupt one's well-being because it prevents individuals from being their true selves. While we all seek acceptance, not everyone will embrace us—Jesus himself experienced rejection.

Authenticity involves recognizing human limitations and accepting that perfection is a myth; ideal human perfection exists only in God. You should strive to be the unique version of yourself, as individuality is crucial. Your tongue prints, iris scans, and fingerprints are peculiar to you.

Being authentic involves understanding your strengths, weaknesses, and areas for improvement. Accepting all parts of yourself, good and bad, is essential for self-growth. How you treat yourself reflects how others will treat you, so choosing positive words and identifiers that resonate with your identity is important. **You cannot nurture what you don't love or acknowledge.**

Genuine authenticity requires aligning your actions with your core values. Deviating from this alignment can evoke feelings of discomfort or guilt. Embracing your imperfections fosters an openness to feedback, which can catalyze personal growth and development.

Feedback and rebuke from God and loved ones are forms of discipline that promote growth, while humility encourages a teachable attitude. Recognizing your identity provides freedom from the chains of imitation. Jesus exemplified humility, learning, and growth despite His divine nature.

To become the best version of yourself, let go of anything that hinders your growth. Forgive yourself and others, and recognize that not everyone will accept you. Authenticity requires vulnerability in safe, supportive spaces. Don't take yourself too seriously; embrace grace during your missteps and build a mindset that rejects condemnation, which inhibits genuine authenticity.

Gratitude
Accepting the reality of your situation can help you appreciate the goodness you've received and the chance to improve things. I'm learning to value the not-so-good because everything works for my benefit. As stated in Chapter 11, make appreciation a lifestyle and practice gratitude daily by focusing on what you have and stop lamenting what you don't have. Lamenting will impact your rest.

Self-compassion
Being patient with yourself involves demonstrating self-empathy, self-kindness, and self-compassion. Healing is a journey that shouldn't be rushed, as it can lead to recurring patterns, yet it shouldn't be prolonged by spending excessive time trying to erase the pain. It's not about how far you go but how well you progress. It's perfectly fine not to have all the answers right now; some may reveal themselves to you later. Soren Kierkegaard, a poet and author, once stated, "Life can only be understood backward, but it must be lived forward."

Embrace a humanistic approach by acknowledging your limitations and accepting yourself for who you are. Avoid dwelling on your past or mistakes; redirect your focus to the opportunities in your present and future.

The inability to show kindness and compassion to oneself often stems from a lack of authenticity. Being kind and compassionate towards yourself fosters the humility needed to receive forgiveness from God, which you can then extend to yourself as you accept your actions with understanding.

Cognitive triad
Be mindful of your thoughts, words, and actions towards yourself and others, especially when you're hungry, angry, lonely, tired (HALT), or sad. Negative self-talk can create self-fulfilling prophecies and lead to self-doubt. Franklin D. Roosevelt Jr., an American lawyer and businessman, noted, "The only limit to our realization of tomorrow will be our doubt of today."

Your body may fail, but your mind remains powerful. Strengthening your mindset is key to achieving your goals. **Remember that your interactions with others, including those you marry or employ, reflect their mindsets. Mental transformation influences your words and actions, determining how far you can go in life.**

Perfection paralysis
God created us to be interdependent and interconnected, so no one is entirely self-made. Acknowledge the all-or-nothing

mindset that drives the pursuit of perfection. Choose progress and improvement over perfection; no one is perfect!

Be aware of impostor syndrome, which tends to arise when you focus on yourself rather than the impact you can make. Don't let others' perceptions of you dictate your potential. Instead, leverage your strengths and take ownership of any areas of low confidence as opportunities for improvement. Everyone is entitled to their opinion, but having an opinion doesn't make it true. As Brené Brown, an American professor and author, said, "You either walk inside your story and own it, or you stand outside your story and hustle for your worthiness." Cultivate and strive to be the best version of yourself that God envisions, not someone else's ideal.

Relationships matter
Critically assess all your relationships and categorize them based on their contribution to your purpose and value function in each pillar of wellness. Family is a fundamental part of our lives, but we cannot choose it. We may have siblings with whom we don't get along or parents who don't share our beliefs or values. However, we can decide how to respond to these situations and how to live our lives. We can choose to let our family's differences define us or rise above them and cultivate our individuality. Ultimately, our attitude toward these situations can impact our overall well-being. By taking responsibility for our thoughts and actions, we can create a more positive and fulfilling life, regardless of our family background. Some relationships are temporary, while others last a lifetime. Problems arise when we force a relationship to

become something it isn't. End relationships that no longer add value to you; they may be draining you. You don't have to create enemies, but you can set healthy boundaries; distance doesn't always have to be permanent. Establishing boundaries based on your values is beneficial as it ensures self-discipline and reduces unhealthy distractions. Another essential reason to heal from emotional wounds is that healing can help prevent unhealthy codependent relationships, often leading to low self-esteem, manipulation, and abuse. Seeking to build relationships focused on strong and supportive connections can promote mutual support, independence, and relationships free from toxic habits.

Don't give power to people who can take it at will, all in the name of validation. Stop seeking external validation and avoid toxic positivity, which can hinder your growth. Don't wait for others to provide you with happy moments. No human relationship will bring 100% satisfaction like the love of God. The love of God offers inner joy that no one can control or take from you. Resting in the love of God will bring contentment. Betrayal is not unique to you. It's not always your fault when someone betrays you; betrayal reflects who the other person is, not who you are. Even our Lord Jesus was betrayed. One day, people shouted, "Hosanna!" but just a few days later, they cried, "Crucify him!" Be vigilant in relationships where betrayal is possible. Observe the patterns and vibes of your relationships. You're either influencing someone or being influenced at every point in life. One of the most important decisions we make in life is choosing our friends. Jesus had many followers and twelve apostles but only three close friends in his inner circle. By following Jesus' example, we can confidently build a supportive and trustworthy circle of friends to help us grow and succeed. Jim Rohn stated, "You are a product of the five people you spend the most time with." **We attract who we are, not who we want. Your relationships reflect who you are.** Don't be with anyone out of fear of being alone. To relate with others, first relate to yourself to discover and understand your values.

Self-care promoters:

Self-Assessment
Begin by completing psychological tests to improve your self-awareness, such as assessing temperament, the OCEAN model (Openness, Conscientiousness, Extroversion, Agreeableness, Neuroticism), and DISC communication styles, etc.

A SWOT analysis (Strengths, Weaknesses, Opportunities, Threats) can help you identify your life's purpose and areas for growth. Harnessing your inherent abilities can provide a significant advantage. Remember, discovering your passions often occurs during challenging times.

Regardless of psychological results, let God's thoughts about you shape your self-image. For example, Gideon was called a "mighty man of valor" despite his weaknesses, and Rahab was part of Jesus' lineage despite her past as a prostitute. Moses, known for his meekness, overcame his history of violence and speech issues, while David was described as "a man after God's own heart" despite his mistakes- adultery and murder. Regardless of your "despite," God ultimately determines your identity.

Commit to a relationship with God.
The higher you rise in life, the deeper and more intimate your relationship with God should become due to the additional responsibilities and worldly affairs that accompany it. In humility, bring all your thoughts and feelings to God; align your thoughts, words, and deeds with God's Word (2 Cor 10:5–6 AMP). Do you need to start or spend more time in devotion—praying, meditating, singing spiritual songs, reading the Bible, fasting, retreating, or serving? Don't procrastinate. Begin today with five minutes of Bible reading. You might start with the book of Genesis or a biblical story. Spend five minutes singing spiritual songs and five minutes in prayer. You can begin by thanking God for His blessings or praying about what's on your heart. As you gain consistency through God's power, you can increase your time. I've learned that the only way to pray is to pray.

Healthy and pleasurable activities
Please don't wait until you feel better to do things because sometimes, you may actually feel better when you engage in activities. Get involved in your hobbies and external activities, such as walking, running, swimming, watching TV, reading a good book, or getting a foot massage. Plan daily activities and future vacations to look forward to. Spend quality time with your family, friends, and God. Pray, sing, dance, read His word, and more.
Participate in activities that make you laugh, as this

releases endorphins and helps you relax. Eat foods rich in the amino acids tyrosine and tryptophan, which break down to form serotonin, such as eggs, chicken, almonds, and bananas.

Stress Relievers

As mentioned in Chapter 2, the sympathetic nervous system activates during stress, while deep breathing engages the parasympathetic nervous system, promoting relaxation by lowering heart rate and blood pressure. It also increases serotonin levels, enhances focus, and reassures the mind of safety. A simple breathing exercise is square breathing (4x4): inhale for 4 seconds, hold for 4 seconds, exhale for 4 seconds, and rest for 4 seconds.

The "5-4-3-2-1" grounding method helps redirect your attention by identifying five things you see, four things you can touch, three sounds, two smells, and one taste, keeping you present during stressful situations. For sleep, try the 4-7-8 technique: inhale for 4 seconds, hold for 7 seconds, and exhale for 8 seconds. Counting backward from 1,000 while breathing can also help focus your mind.

Visualizing your favorite place and paying attention to every detail—the blue of the sky, the texture of the sand, the color of the water, the sounds, and so on—engages your senses and enhances mindfulness. Lastly, practicing a body scan by focusing on and relaxing one area at a time can also be beneficial. You can start from your toes and work your way up to your head, or vice versa.

Goal setting
Break your goals into small, achievable steps. SMART stands for Specific, Measurable, Achievable, Relevant, and Time-bound. This approach is effective for both personal and professional growth. Does your goal encompass spending more time with family, drinking more water, eating healthier foods, taking walks in the sun, or taking a break from social media?

Start today. As the Chinese proverb states, "The best time to plant a tree was 20 years ago, and the second-best time is now." If you need a more comprehensive financial analysis, consider consulting a professional and scheduling a visit with your financial planner. Do you need to advance your education for intellectual growth, career development, or improved time management? If so, consider pursuing courses or seeking professional support.

Observe patterns of success and challenges in your life, and seek guidance from accomplished teachers, mentors, role models, or coaches who align with your values. This can help you save time and avoid unnecessary mistakes.

Routine wellness visits
Schedule routine wellness check-ups with a physician. Regardless of how blessed we are, our spirits still require our bodies to function in this life, just as a car needs maintenance. People of faith often say, "I don't need a doctor." Perhaps the prayer should be that the Lord guides us to the doctor aligned with His heart for us.

We don't rely on faith alone to keep a car running. When a car breaks down, we won't solely pray. We should care for our bodies because they are the tools we use to function here on Earth. Jim Rohn remarked, "Take care of your body. It's the only place you have to live." Take your vitamins and medications while waiting for complete healing.

The church serves as a hospital for the soul and spirit. Both physicians and servants of God are there to help people, not to fix them. Jesus said, "Those who are well have no need of a physician, but those who are sick. I did not come to call *the* righteous, but sinners, to repentance" (Mark 2:17).

Delegation

It's time to face the facts: no one is indispensable, including you. To avoid burnout, delegating responsibilities and tasks as needed is essential. Delegating will free up your time and energy, allowing you to focus on the things that truly matter. As John Maxwell, author, speaker, and founder of Maxwell Leadership, once said, "If you want to do a few small things right, do them yourself. Learn to delegate if you want to do great things and make a big impact." It's crucial to prioritize your tasks to achieve optimal work-life integration. Always remember that if something were to happen to you today, life would continue. Take charge and delegate wisely!

First, be your champion; find your voice and help others do the same.

Perhaps you've discovered your strength, but the reason to help others find theirs is unclear. Flip to the next chapter for the healing benefits of serving others.

CHAPTER FOURTEEN

ACTS OF SERVICE

But whoever desires to become great among you, let him be your servant.

— MATTHEW 20:27

Doctor, "I would prefer to keep to myself because of my suffering; why do I need to help others?" "How can I help others despite my pain and limitations?" "Do I have what it takes to help others?"

Many people aspire to greatness, but few truly understand its meaning or the sacrifices it entails. Greatness is achieved through deliberate pursuit.

One primary key to unlocking your full potential is assisting others. Small acts of kindness can have a significant impact on you and those around you. Giving back is a powerful way to achieve personal growth and make a positive difference in the world.

Mother Teresa, a Catholic nun and missionary, stated, "A life not lived for others is not a life at all." Do you agree or disagree? Or should serving be a one-way street?

Have you wondered why one would want to serve while struggling with their challenges? Our selfishness may think, "Is my life perfect? I'd rather wait until my life is in order before helping others.

Service is not an option for anyone who wants to be great, break a generational cycle of pain, or change the narrative of a generation. We live by selflessly making a positive difference in others' lives, no matter how small.

You can serve others with any ability, including your hobbies, acquired skills, expertise, gifts, or talent. This doesn't exclude what most people refer to as a disability, which is a different ability that can be refined to help others.

The science of service

Service to others has shown multiple psychological benefits in several studies, including:

- Positive emotions and reduction of depression
- Greater health as it reduces blood pressure
- Increased longevity by reducing stress level
- Improved social and relational skills
- Better relationships
- Advanced career

- Fun and relaxation
- Increased confidence
- Fulfilled life

The concept of "helper's high" emerged in the 1980s and has been confirmed in numerous studies since then. It consists of positive emotions following selfless service to others. Greater health and increased longevity are associated with this psychological state.

Service is associated with the release of the neurotransmitters dopamine and serotonin. When we care for one another, stress hormones are reduced. However, the opposite occurs when we serve out of pressure or when we don't see a positive impact in our service, leading to depressed mood and increased stress levels.

Altruism

Altruism is one of the mature psychological defense mechanisms of the ego that balances the unrealistic conflicts between the id and super-id. Merriam-Webster defines altruism as "an unselfish regard for or the devotion to the welfare of others." In psychology, helping others brings a sense of internal satisfaction. Our interactions and environments influence it. **Like many behaviors, altruism can be modeled in children and others around us.**

Psychologists have identified four types of altruism:

1. Genetic: altruistic acts that benefit close family members
2. Reciprocal: altruistic acts focused on give and take relationship
3. Group selected: altruistic acts for people based on groups of affiliation, the shared or common benefit of a particular group
4. Pure: this is referred to as moral altruism, motivated by internalized values and morals without any expectation of a reward

A significant danger of altruism and service is the potential to overlook one's own health—physical, psychological, financial, occupational, social, environmental, spiritual, and intellectual—and the risk of entitlement and manipulation.

Genuine service

Genuine service is not about making you look good or better than anyone else. Instead, the purpose of service is for God to reach others through us (2 Corinthians 9:12–15).

This kind of service is not intended to be repaid by the same person. You don't hold the person at ransom for your good deed. God-centered service may be the most rewarding because only God can genuinely reward your worth on earth and in heaven.

Genuine service is not self-centered or focused on manipulation; otherwise, you would lose relationships and blessings. True service may be for those who can never thank you.

"And if you do good to those who do good to you, what credit is that to you? For even sinners do the same. And if you lend to those from whom you hope to receive back, what credit is that to you? For even sinners lend to sinners to receive as much back."

— (LUKE 6:33–34)

Service is not about public recognition or the quantity or size of what you do. More importantly, it's about the purity of your heart in terms of pleasing God and selflessness. Service should not only be seasonal; we should always serve moment-to-moment.

Service involves any assistance we can offer to another person to improve their life.

Charles Dickens, an English novelist, stated, "No one is useless in this world who lightens the burdens of others."

Service involves raising our children or providing mentorship and discipleship to the next generation so that their outcomes will be better than ours. It brings glory to God and transformation to others and nations.

If people, including parents, view the help and support they provide to those in their care from this perspective, it may reduce the sense of entitlement and abuse (abnormal use) of their children. It may reduce the mindset centered on "After all I have done for you." It may also help to focus on giving primarily to serve others rather than expecting repayment from those we help; instead, we should be content with the knowledge that God is our reward.

We are privileged to be the stewards of children, relationships, and the blessings God has given us. God treasures whatever good we show anyone (Matthew 25:40).

You may achieve success through your accomplishments, but you can only be truly significant by serving others. Mark Cole, the CEO of John Maxwell Enterprise, stated, "Success is what happens to you, but significance is what happens to others through you." God has a different operating system for greatness. Service is God's strategy for turning potential into reality. In God's kingdom, the servant is the greatest.

Servant leadership

Service is a cornerstone of effective leadership. When we think of leadership, it's essential to recognize that it's not about being served by others but rather about being of service to others. The highest leadership style focuses on serving others and equipping them to reach their full potential. It's also referred to as servant leadership. An anonymous quote stated, "If serving others is below you, then leadership is beyond you."

Servant leadership is selfless, as it prioritizes the well-being of those around it. Most leaders are not aware that leadership is a form of service. One can achieve servant leadership through delegation, mentorship, identifying opportunities to help others, and even leading by example.

ACTS OF SERVICE

Servant- leaders inspire trust, integrity, and respect in others. They don't need a title attached to their names. They start by leading themselves first before leading others. John Maxwell stated, "Selfish people seldom find significance; when you help others, you help yourself. When you help yourself, you may not help others."

God established systems and principles to prevent selfishness. God made us value interdependence and interconnection to prevent self-sufficiency by creating areas in our lives that depend on service and support from others. God blessed us so we can be a blessing to others. **There are skills we possess that may not directly benefit us but would help others through us.**

Sometimes, we try to manipulate the system by seeking to serve the people we would like to bless or to have them serve us in return, without realizing that God didn't say we would be rewarded by the same person or place we serve. God wants us to trust Him as the faithful rewarder (Hebrews 11:6).

QUALITIES OF GENUINE SERVICE INSPIRED BY THE LIFE OF JESUS CHRIST

Selflessness

Jesus' service was motivated by His love for God, and our goal should be to glorify Him rather than seek personal recognition. In our roles as parents, friends, or professionals, we should strive to honor God in all that we do (Colossians

3:17). Our service should emanate from love and a desire to please God, thereby strengthening our relationship with Him.

It's essential to distinguish between working for God and walking with Him. While we may eagerly volunteer in church activities, we must also prioritize intimate time with God.

Our motivation for serving Him should be to please, honor, and partner with Him. The intention behind our actions is just as significant as the action itself. We must not allow service to replace or distract us from our relationship with God.

Genuine Love for Others

Jesus teaches us to love others as He loves us (John 15:9–13), a standard that surpasses the one in Mark 12:31. True service is about making a positive impact, rather than seeking personal gain. We must ensure we genuinely care for those we serve, especially the vulnerable. As Rick Warren said, "Selflessness is not thinking less of yourself but thinking of yourself less."

Compassion

Jesus illustrated compassion through His acts of kindness (Matthew 14:14–16). We need to receive God's love and mercy to extend kindness to others. Everyone needs kindness; it doesn't take too much to be kind. We must first receive God's love, compassion, and gentleness before we can give them to others.

Commitment

Jesus remained committed to His purpose despite facing challenges (Luke 22:42; Hebrews 12:2). This commitment makes it easier to share and spread love to others. Fulfilling one's purpose always involves giving oneself to others; purpose never ends with the individual. For example, can a bottle drink by itself, or can a dress wear itself?

Theodore Roosevelt Jr., the 26th President of the United States, said, "People don't care how much you know until they know how much you care." Love is a powerful tool for change, while condemnation can lead to harm. Love serves as a universal language.

Sacrifice

Service detaches you from your possessions as you realize you're only a steward. Service may not always cost us our lives, as it did for Jesus, but it may cost us our time, attention, or support. "While we were still sinners, Christ died for us" (Romans 5:8). There is no love without giving something, reminding us that we are stewards of what we possess.

Humility

Humility is intentional and based on how God sees us rather than the world's perspective. It involves submitting to learning and recognizing our need for God's grace (Romans 3:23). Our flaws help us connect with others (2 Corinthians 10:12). Emotional pain can make us selfish and proud, leading us to fear looking foolish or weak. It's essential to distinguish between genuine humility and being exploited.

Service requires openness to teaching and mentorship, as exemplified by David's learning from King Saul in the Bible.

Diligence
Jesus was dedicated to His mission, consistently working to bring glory to God and investing in others through personal and servant leadership. He taught and mentored His disciples before His death. After His resurrection, Jesus did not immediately ascend to Heaven. Although He had accomplished His primary purpose—to become our wisdom, sanctification, redemption, and righteousness to God (1 Corinthians 1:30)—He remained on the earth for an additional forty days. During this time, He prepared the disciples for the arrival of the Holy Spirit and the global revival that would follow.

BENEFITS OF SERVICE FROM THE BIBLE

God rewards genuine commitment to service. As Olajumoke Adenowo stated, "Service is both a mandate and a privilege from God." Serving others is an investment that yields multiple rewards across all areas of wellness.

Here are some benefits:

> Multiplication and Increase (Matthew 25:29): Those who wisely use their gifts receive even more. The Shunamite woman's service to Prophet Elisha, in providing a small room, led to her being blessed with

a son (2 Kings 4:8-37), demonstrating that genuine service can bring unexpected rewards.

Influence: Diligent service can open doors to more significant opportunities and influence (Luke 19:17). God rewarded Jesus for His sacrifice with the highest honor (Acts 4:12, Philippians 2:9–11).

Generational Blessings: Service can create blessings that benefit future generations and lead to lasting impact, as shown by Hur's support of Moses, leading to favor for his grandson Bezalel (Exodus 17; 30:1-3)

Increased Capacity and Spiritual Empowerment: Prophet Elisha received a double portion of blessings after serving Elijah, illustrating how dedication can transform our lives.

Opportunities and Promotion: Joseph served using his gift of interpreting dreams while in prison and was eventually promoted to Pharaoh's second-in-command.

Positive Relationships: Ruth remained loyal to Naomi and was rewarded with marriage to Boaz, thereby connecting her to King David and ultimately to Jesus. Rebecca's service to Abraham's servant ultimately led to her marriage to Isaac.

Preservation: Rahab helped the spies and was spared from Jericho's destruction, while Naaman was healed through the guidance of the Israelite girl.

Transformation: Service can lead to personal growth and a sense of purpose, as Esther discovered on her journey from being a slave to becoming a queen. Serving others helps shift our perspective and purpose. Esther's journey from a slave girl to a queen is a testament to how God-honoring service transforms lives.

Pastor Bolaji Idowu, the lead pastor of Harvesters International Church, stated, "Life is not about accumulation but contribution. There are things you do not pray into but serve into." A man's life doesn't consist of the abundance of things he possesses.

Serving others can turn our pain into purpose. The lessons we learn from our suffering can benefit others in their struggles. When your pain helps someone else, it loses its power over you. This is the transformative impact of service—it converts personal challenges into tools for assisting others. If we follow God's will and honor Jesus instead of seeking our pleasure, God will reward us, for He does not forget our sacrifices of love (Hebrews 6:10, Hebrews 13:16).

Serving transforms what could have brought harm into a survival guide for others.

Joyce Meyer, a Christian author and the president of Joyce Meyer Ministries, stated,

I was sexually, mentally, emotionally, and verbally abused by my father as far back as I can remember, until I left home at the age of 18. He did many terrible things...some of which are too distasteful for me to talk about publicly. But I want to share my testimony because so many people have been hurt, and they need to realize that someone has made it through their struggles so they can have hope.

Pastor Joyce Meyer uses her testimony to inspire others to believe that recovery and healing through God are possible. She serves as a great example of how one can transform misery into ministry and a mess into a message. Indeed, God comforts us so we can comfort others (2 Corinthians 1:3–5). Through our light, others can discover their light.

At this point, you may be sure that no experience is wasted and have learned the outstanding benefits of service, but it may be challenging for you to ask for help in your time of need. The next chapter will provide valuable resources.

CHAPTER FIFTEEN

SUPPORT SYSTEM

Bear one another's burdens, and so fulfill the law of Christ.

— GALATIANS 6:2

Doctor, "Why do I need support?" "Why do I struggle with asking for help?" "Do strong people still need help?"

What comes to your mind when you hear the word "support"?

Some people view support as a thing of weakness and shame. Many people are ashamed to ask for support due to cultural, social, or personal biases. Some think support is primarily financial.

According to Merriam-Webster, support is defined as "to endure bravely or quietly, or to promote the interests or cause of." While several societies encourage self-sufficiency and the development of attitudes that do not rely on others, the expectation in psychology is the opposite.

Support is not gender specific. It's a basic human need. The support system consists of people you can turn to in your time of need and crisis. These people are interested in your well-being. They may include spouses, siblings, parents, children, friends, colleagues, neighbors, and divine helpers, among others.

In Christianity, particularly in Africa, the term "divine or destiny helper" refers to someone who is connected to one's destiny and supports them in fulfilling God's purpose for their life. This person collaborates with your efforts to achieve that purpose and may not necessarily be someone within your immediate circle.

Abraham Maslow, an American Psychologist, developed the five-level hierarchy of needs as a theory of human motivation, often displayed as a pyramid that includes physiological (1st level), safety (2nd level), and psychological needs that lead to self-actualization. Psychological needs consist of the 3rd level (Belonging and love) and the 4th level (self-esteem). Belonging refers to a human emotional need for interpersonal relationships, connectedness, and being part of a group and community. It includes family, acceptance, trust, friendship, and intimacy.

The desire to belong to a group is a universal and inherent aspect of human nature. When this desire is not fulfilled, it leads to emotional difficulties in forming relationships. You're at risk for loneliness, isolation, anxiety, and depression.

Our relationships are so meaningful that Harry Stack Sullivan, an American psychiatrist, developed the interpersonal theory of personality and psychiatry. This theory focuses on interpersonal relationships and the effects of the social and cultural environment on inner life rather than on innate drives[1]. It also explains the role of interpersonal interactions in meeting needs, reducing anxiety, and shaping personality.[2]

Interpersonal therapy (IPT) explores the effect of maladaptive thoughts and behaviors on interpersonal relationships. Poor interpersonal skills and interactions can break down relationships and social support.

A lack of social support is one of the risk factors for suicide. Whenever someone reports suicidal thoughts, a mental health professional must assess their suicide risk and safety plan. One of the key components of this assessment involves asking the person about their support system during a crisis.

Bobby Genovese, a Businessman and the founder of BG Capital Group Limited, stated, "People want to be heard and loved. That attitude of acceptance and support inspires them to be the best they can be."

THE SCIENCE OF SOCIAL SUPPORT

Social support is the care or help we receive from others. Social support can affect our physical and mental health and behavior patterns, thereby leading to the prevention, development, and management of mental health disorders such as depression and other health problems, including hypertension.

Strong social support is a protective factor during stressful times, whereas social isolation can hurt both mental and physical health.

Maya Angelou, an American civil rights activist, stated, "I've learned that people will forget what you said, people will forget what you did, but people will never forget how you made them feel."

Research has shown that feelings of loneliness typically occur when individuals spend 75% or more of their time alone, highlighting the distinction between being alone and experiencing loneliness.[3] Unfortunately, loneliness has become a significant issue since the COVID-19 pandemic that began in 2020, which involved social distancing.

Loneliness can lead to low-quality social relationships. The W.H.O. has referred to loneliness as a pressing health threat and recently launched a new commission to address loneliness and promote social connection in all countries.

Stress is a common part of life, but excessive stress can hurt various aspects of our lives. One of the key pillars of wellness is social well-being, which is closely linked to our overall well-being, encompassing physical, mental, emotional, financial, environmental, intellectual, spiritual, and occupational aspects. **Lack of social wellness can hinder our ability to lead a fulfilling life.**

It's important to remember that many people, even those who appear strong or are also Christians, may be suffering in silence. Let us treat others with kindness and understanding, just as we would like to be treated. After all, life can change in an instant, and no one has a perfect life.

Living by the Golden Rule—treating others as you would like to be treated (Matthew 7:12)—can inspire those around you and have a profoundly positive impact on the world. This principle emphasizes empathy, respect, and consideration in our interactions with others.

We should remember life is in seasons; no condition is permanent. While we seek, pray, and trust God for support, God encourages connections and interdependence. God honors the law of sowing and reaping, which can be applied to support one's efforts. God provides support to human beings through the help of one another.

Support should not always be one-sided. While others help you when you're in need, you should strive to help others when they're in need as well.

You cannot do life alone. Support may include people, medication, prayers, money, etc. It should never overtake your life. It takes courage to ask for help and strength to receive it. True strength lies in building resilience, recognizing when to seek help, and persisting until you receive it. Support may be short—or long-term.

Life is a marathon—not a race to be run alone. I imagine life as a driver in a motorsports race, with people offering support through tire pressure adjustments, fuel, new tires, mechanical fixes, and refreshments along the way until you reach the finish line. Alternatively, a driver may change during their pause at the pit stop and eventually return to the race.

Since unhealed emotional pain can make us selfish and fearful, it may prevent us from sowing seeds of kindness, acceptance, value, and love for others. Unfortunately, the negative mindset of rejection and loneliness becomes reinforced when we don't receive help from those we expected or feel entitled to help, thereby making us more isolated within our self-imposed walls.

Living an isolated Christian life won't benefit you in the days of adversity. Our lives will be disastrous if we allow our emotions to drive or lead our Christian lives. **No human being, regardless of status, is meant to live life alone.** Dependence on yourself alone will cause you to become overwhelmed by your problem(s).

TYPES OF SUPPORT

People often think money is the only kind of support. Here are other types of support to consider:

Time

It's one of the most expensive commodities. Time is the unit of life. Once spent, it cannot be recovered. Asking for another person's time can be the most challenging, especially when it's not paid for, as you're asking that person to set aside their agenda for you. This may include various other types of support, such as emotional support and physical presence. The assurance of our availability may be the most beneficial to someone grieving, as it gives them space to grieve.

Energy

Energy can be physical, social, intellectual, or emotional in nature. It may include strategic planning, physical assistance, or advocacy on behalf of another person.

Words

This includes offering encouraging words or pep talks to boost courage and hope in yourself or someone around you. Sometimes, it may be counsel, including constructive criticism. This approach may be effective when someone is grieving a situation, person, or outcome while avoiding the urge to rescue or fix the person. "Pleasant words *are like* a honeycomb, Sweetness to the soul and health to the bones" (Proverbs 16:24).

Prayers/Intercession

Sometimes, we may need others to pray for us for various reasons.

"Pray for one another, that you may be healed *and* restored.

The heartfelt *and* persistent prayer of a righteous man (believer) can accomplish much [when put into action and made effective by God—it is dynamic and can have tremendous power]" (James 5:16 AMP).

Finance/Funds
Money is the most common support people need or think of, but it may be one of the least important. Money can buy a lot, but there are so many things money cannot buy. If you ask a dying man, money may not be his most significant concern, as time may be his most cherished wish. The rich may crave human and social connection the most or a better relationship with their children.
Who can you call during a crisis? Have you sown seeds of love, kindness, acceptance, connections, trust, and dependability in others?

PRACTICAL LESSONS ABOUT SUPPORT IN THE BIBLE

The New Testament emphasizes the significance of support through our Lord Jesus. While He is fully God and entirely sufficient on His own, He chose to embody humanity (Hebrews 2:17) to demonstrate our essential need for support from both God and one another.

- Jesus relied on God while on earth.

    I can do nothing on my own initiative or authority. Just as I hear, I judge; and My judgment is just (fair, right-

eous, unbiased), because I do not seek My own will, but only the will of Him who sent Me.

— (JOHN 5:30, AMP)

- Jesus was financially supported by several women for His ministry on earth. These were women to whom He had shown compassion and mercy by healing them of their illnesses and delivering them from demonic oppression (Luke 8:2–3).

- Simon of Cyrene physically supported Jesus with the cross when He was exhausted (Mark 15:21).

- After Jesus' death, Joseph of Arimathea supported him. Along with Nicodemus, Joseph requested Jesus' body and prepared it for burial (John 19:38–40).

- After His resurrection, Jesus chose men to spread the gospel across the nations.

If Jesus' humanity serves as an example for us, we must acknowledge that we cannot survive without the support of God and others during our time on earth.

GOD'S SYSTEM OF SUPPORT

Apostle Joshua Selman often states, "All blessings come from God but come through men to men." Whatever you need is on this earth, but God shows you kindness through the help of others. Humans are selfish by nature. It's essential to manage your expectations when others make choices that benefit themselves but negatively impact you. If someone thinks of you and is committed to your success and well-being, it's more than natural thoughtfulness; it's a supernatural influence.

Although God wants us to be interdependent, He detests 100% reliance on another human (Jeremiah 17:5). Several scriptures in the Bible speak about God being our helper (Psalm 46:1–3). God is called "Abba Father," one of His significant names, based on His relationship with us. "Abba" is an Aramaic word meaning "Father." A Father means "Source."

You never want to reach a point where you become too strong, intelligent, or advanced to rely on God for your needs, as the rich fool did (Luke 12:16–21).

We must be rooted in Jesus for growth, transformation, and fruitfulness; otherwise, our selfishness will always take control, leading to disaster (John 15:5).

Jesus taught that love and mercy are demonstrated through support for our neighbor, as seen in the parable of the Good Samaritan in Luke 10:25–37. The injured man was ignored by a Levite and the priest or God-professing people like you and me. Thank God for the Samaritan who was so kind.

How can we provide support if not first supported or secured?

SUPPORT SYSTEM

You wouldn't lack support if you sowed unselfishly because seed and harvest time won't cease due to the law of sowing and reaping. The same rule applies if you sowed evil to others or didn't sow at all except by the mercy of God. Let us be mindful and intentional about sowing, including what we sow and how we do it. God can send you help from another place beyond your understanding or reach (Luke 6:38, Isaiah 46:11).

Regardless of background, faith, or other factors, our relationships should be characterized by total dependence on God and interdependence with one another. It's not IF we need help but WHEN we need help.

I agree that a threefold cord is great in marriage (Ecclesiastes 4:9–12). However, this verse applies not only to marriage but also to all relationships. **Support is essential because you will fall sometimes, and others will fall, too.**

It's better to establish a support system before you need it rather than waiting until you're in crisis. It would be best if you nurtured it before demanding it. Your relationship with God also involves sustenance and provision, which make you stronger and increase your capacity to help others. Have you invested in a relationship with God and with humankind?

Some people want to withdraw funds from an account they have not invested in. Some approach God only when they need something. We should not use God or people. Success may be impossible without strategic relationships, self-actualization, and purpose deployment. Several people in history have risen from nothing to significance because of their leverage on relationships. Relationships are meaningful because they contribute to your wisdom or foolishness (Proverbs 13:20).

Ignoring human interaction and relationships reflects a lack of wisdom. The world encourages self-sufficiency, but it doesn't yield true wisdom. God didn't create a self-sufficient system.

We cannot achieve many things without a valuable or strategic support relationship.

Les Brown, an American motivational speaker, said, "Ask for support. Not because you are weak but because you want to remain strong." We are not always able to do all things ourselves. There are things money can buy and things money cannot buy.

Many people have not risen or advanced because of their lack of a valuable or strategic relationship, as seen in the Bible, 'The sick man answered Him, "Sir, I have no man to put me into the pool when the water is stirred up; but while I am coming, another steps down before me"' (John 5:7).

Compare this with the story of the paralyzed man who was carried by friends to Jesus to be healed, as they lowered him through the roof of the house where Jesus was teaching at the time (Mark 2:3–4).

There is often a human being behind the results that God brings about on earth (Psalms 115:16). The Israelites were in slavery for 430 years—30 years longer than the 400 years previously prophesied (Genesis 15:13). Deliverance from slavery did not occur until Moses had matured and was ready to lead.

It was not God who directly appeared before Pharaoh but Moses, who God empowered. Even people of influence, such as kings, are not exempt from needing human support (Proverbs 14:28). Therefore, all hope is never lost for those who have the backing of others.

COMMON BARRIERS TO ASKING OR PROVIDING HELP

Individual attachment type

Attachment theory was developed by John Bowlby, a psychologist, who examined human relationships and the bonds between infants and caregivers. Bowlby believed that as infants grow, they seek comfort and resources to survive from caregivers, especially during times of fear. This early relationship influences attachment styles that can persist into adulthood and throughout life.

Mary Ainsworth, a psychologist, expanded on this theory through her "Strange Situation" study, where she identified three attachment styles in infants based on their behavior during reunions after separation:

- Secure: The infant cried and was comforted upon reuniting with the parent.
- Anxious-ambivalent-insecure: The infant was conflicted between being comforted by the parent

and showing anger towards the parent when reunited.
- Avoidant-insecure: The infant avoided the parent and played with objects instead of reuniting with the parent.

Mary Main and Judith Solomon, psychologists, developed the fourth one.

- Fearful-avoidant-disorganized-insecure: The Infant approached the caregiver but retreated in fear, indicating a lack of trust.

In adulthood, attachment styles impact how individuals form relationships and handle intimacy. These styles may stem from a fear of rejection, a preference for self-sufficiency, or a need for interpersonal boundaries. Attachment styles influence relationships with oneself (self-love and worthiness) and others (the ability to depend on others during stressful times).

Bartholomew and Horowitz, psychologists, identified four adult attachment styles:

1. Secure: Comfortable expressing emotions and able to rely on others.[4]
2. Preoccupied: A negative self-image but a positive view of others, seeking validation through relationships. This style stems from the anxious-ambivalent-insecure attachment developed during infancy.

3. Dismissive: This person has a positive self-image but a negative view of others. They struggle to form lasting connections due to their fear of intimacy.[5] This style stems from an avoidant-insecure attachment established during infancy.
4. Fearful-Avoidant-Disorganized-Insecure: Negative self-image and distrust towards others, often struggling with intimacy and potentially sabotaging calm relationships, leading to a pattern of chaos. This usually stems from a fearful-avoidant or disorganized attachment style developed in infancy, typically influenced by a chaotic or toxic upbringing.

They become suspicious when they have a calm and secure relationship. They may provoke or accuse the partner of creating chaos, a behavior that is more familiar and may lead to the termination of the relationship.

Unfortunately, we project our attachment styles onto God, which, if not secure, may affect our dependence and trust in God. It may lead to relationships that are avoidant, dismissive, and transactional, prioritizing our needs over relational intimacy.

Recognizing your emotions and feelings can help you become more self-aware of your attachment style. Understanding these attachment styles can promote personal growth. It is essential to bring your hurts and pain from your past to God to be healed. If you struggle with low self-esteem and an inability to trust God and others for support, your experiences with parents, caregivers, and the environment may have contributed to this. It is best to seek the truth about yourself courageously, despite your negative feelings, multiple perspectives or popular opinion, by understanding God's nature and unconditional love and rising above lies.

Lack of knowledge
Imagine if Jesus had died on the ground due to a lack of human support. The curse may not have been broken because He was meant to die on the cross to become the curse for us. **Knowledge of ourselves and our limitations as human beings may help us recognize there is a season to ask for help and a season to be the help to others. No season is permanent.** You never know the potential of who you have the opportunity to help today. We should know that both God and the devil can use humans for our upliftment or downfall, respectively.

Pride
Many people view asking for help as a sign of weakness, and we don't want others to perceive us as weak. Anyone who looks down on another doesn't understand that no condition is permanent. It could be your turn tomorrow because money and riches fail and fly away.
Well, I can tell you, as a physician, during childbirth, I could not help myself. I needed the support of the nurses, another physician, and staff to help me with multiple things. Sometimes, we become suddenly dependent on others for necessities. If Jesus was not exempt from this while He lived on earth, we should accept this as a reality.

Pride can also explain the other extreme of asking from an entitled mentality. Whenever you ask for something based on your rights, you're no longer asking for help but making a demand. Demand and help differ in that the former asks for something you're owed, while the latter is for assistance and support. You're entitled to your salary, but no one owes you help. Imagine an adult who should be independent, demanding your resources as if it's their right. I would advise that when you need assistance, don't demand support from others but ask in humility; otherwise, you may discourage your helper to your detriment.

Emotional pain
You may hesitate to seek help due to past disappointments or rejections. Since disappointment often arises from unmet expectations, does your expectation exceed your contribution to the relationship—are you a self-centered person? Does your contribution exceed your withdrawal? Do people take advantage of you?

Fear
Some people don't seek help or help others because they fear potential negative consequences, such as ridicule, criticism, jest, public sharing, poor management of the help provided, manipulation, and entitlement from those seeking support. Unfortunately, everything in life carries a level of risk due to the fear of the unknown.
One thing that may reduce the magnitude of fear is seeking God's direction and guidance from both parties—the seeker

and the provider of help. While God understands our concerns, He rewards those who obey His counsel. Courage is not the absence of fear but rather doing something despite the fear. If you ignore human beings, you may pay a considerable sacrifice. **Human beings are ladders and bridges that can leverage your life and destiny. Relationships are like investments.**

Culture

Due to certain socio-cultural beliefs and perceptions, asking for help is often perceived as a sign of weakness and shame. This makes it harder for people to speak up or ask for help, even for health challenges, including mental illness. Racial or ethnic groups, such as Asians, tend to view a person as connected to others, while Westerners tend to view an individual as independent and separate.[6]

In some countries, there are concerns about the generational stigma surrounding mental health concerns and illnesses. As a result, individuals with mental health challenges and their families are often treated with disdain. Many men have either died due to these pressures or choose to remain silent and stagnant out of shame. Societal factors may contribute to the lower reported rates of mental illness among men compared to women. Additionally, feelings of shame may help explain why men are two to four times more likely to die by suicide, while women are two to three times more likely to attempt suicide than men.

SUPPORT SYSTEM

I saw a video on social media of a man holding a sign asking for someone to talk to him because he has anxiety and depression. Not one person stopped to ask or check on him. However, when the same man held a sign that read "free money," he was flooded with people who took the money within seconds of seeing his message. It was a sad reality of life to behold.

BENEFITS OF SUPPORTING OTHERS

Regardless of the type of support, it should be done by God's will and to honor Jesus rather than for personal gain. Here are some benefits to keep in mind:

Multiplication and Enlarged Capacity
This was evident in the biblical story of Naomi and Ruth, as stated in Chapter 13.

Harvest of Support in Your Time of Need
This principle is taught by the story of Rahab and the two spies in the Bible (Judges 2). Rahab protected the two Israelite spies during their exploration of Jericho, and in return, she and her family were spared when the Israelites conquered the city. Another biblical example is Naaman, a brave soldier and army commander who suffered from leprosy. He was kind to a slave girl, and in turn, she referred him to the Prophet Elisha for healing from leprosy (2 Kings 5).

Generational Blessings
According to the Bible, Jonathan loved David deeply (1

Samuel 18:1) and showed him kindness. Despite being the son of King Saul and the rightful heir to the throne, Jonathan didn't fight David for power; instead, he defended and protected David from his father's anger, which could have led to death. After Jonathan's death, David honored their friendship by sparing the life of Jonathan's son, Mephibosheth, and showed favor (I Samuel 9:1–13, 2 Samuel 21).

WAYS TO ACHIEVE OR MAINTAIN VALUABLE AND STRATEGIC RELATIONSHIPS

"A man *who has* friends must himself be friendly."

— (PROVERBS 18:24)

Avoid jealousy
Maintaining a strategic relationship is impossible with jealousy and envy (Proverbs 14:30). Some individuals focus on being the center of attention, needing to be the only significant ones. Otherwise, they become destructive or refuse to offer their support.

Avoid assumptions
Making assumptions can destroy relationships. Henry Winkler, an American actor and author, said, "Assumptions are the termites of relationships." It's important to be curious, ask questions, and remain nonjudgmental to clarify assumptions.

Practice kindness

There is no kindness without giving. Don't look down on anyone because you never know whose help you may need in the future. This can be learned through practice. Kindness is about being generous and considerate of others. It also involves spreading hope and smiles throughout your life. Carl Sagan, an American astrophysicist, stated, "Let us temper criticism with kindness. None of us comes fully equipped." When we witness others' hardships or misfortunes, we should refrain from judging, laughing, rejoicing, or gloating (Obadiah 1:12). This doesn't please God, who is the God of justice and mercy. I encourage you to repent if you've made fun of others.

Avoid evil speaking and backbiting

Evil speaking and backbiting can cause chaos and easily strain any relationship. You cannot afford to speak evil of others if you want a strategic relationship that builds up rather than tears down (Galatians 5:15). Eleanor Roosevelt, First Lady of the 32nd President of the United States, stated, "Great minds discuss ideas; average minds discuss events; small minds discuss people."

Practice forgiveness and tolerance

Be an active contributor to fostering strong relationships. Valuable relationships are typically built over time, not overnight. This typically involves mutual connection, communication, contribution, and mutual expectation. An unhealthy balance between contribution and expectation can lead to abuse, entitlement, bitterness, selfishness, and co-dependence. Avoid or leave any abusive relationship that can be damaging, stressful, and destructive.

Find ways to be the support you wish you had from others. Lailah Gifty Akita, a Ghanaian author, stated, "There are moments of frustration in life. It would help if you built good relations to support you in these moments. You must also learn to encourage yourself and decide to stay determined in life."

Remember this: **Seeking support is crucial, but being the one to provide support is even more encouraging. Be the reason why someone smiles today.**

CONCLUSION

Adversity is common to humanity, and faith doesn't make anyone immune to emotional pain. Instead, faith provides an advantage and renews hope for a good outcome. Unhealed psychological pain can impact all your senses and every aspect of your life, and addressing it requires authenticity, courage, humility, and an openness to receiving help.

Give your pain meaning that fosters growth, not stagnation or decay.

It's important to know who you are, whose you are, and why you were created. Everyone has different opinions about you, shaped by culture, experiences, and expectations. God's opinion is the most important one that counts with your permission.

Your words reflect your heart and, ultimately, who you are. The Bible is a powerful tool for healing, growth, and transfor-

CONCLUSION

mation. Prayer is for everyone, and forgiveness is a gift you give to yourself and others by letting go of your desire for retaliation.

An attitude of gratitude promotes growth and intelligence, while music can shift your mindset and emotions from negative to positive and vice versa.

One song, prayer, or verse can cause a mindset and emotional shift from negativity to positivity.

Serving others is our gift to God, and we should focus on bringing glory to Him.

A wise person doesn't suffer in silence or act as if they can do it alone. Instead, they recognize their need for help, seek it, and don't quit until they've found and received it. And then support others to do likewise. Let us normalize and foster seeking help as a sign of courage, not weakness.

Use the tools in this book to **ADAPT-FAITH™** to any situation:

- A: Acknowledge your emotions and thoughts.
- D: Discover God's word, prayer, and practice.
- A: Ask for lessons and adopt a mindset shift.
- P: Prioritize what you can control and trust God with what you can't.
- T: Take responsibility for your actions and reactions.

These steps will guide your healing, but they're most effec-

CONCLUSION

tive when applied. Use the companion workbook to reflect, journal, and track your progress on this personal journey.

Remember, "The end of a thing is better than its beginning; the patient in spirit is better than the proud in spirit" (Ecclesiastes 7:8).

FAITH-BASED FAQS

HOW DO I BEGIN TO KNOW JESUS?

You can start by speaking these statements aloud and believing in your heart (Romans 10:9–13):

> Lord Jesus, today, I confess that I believe You are the Son of God.
> I believe You died for me and rose again for my righteousness.
> Right now, I confess You are the savior of my soul and the Lord of my life.
> I declare that the power of sin, Satan, hell, and grave is broken over my life.
> I receive Your unconditional love for me and Your gift of eternal life in Jesus' name.
> Amen.

Please write or memorize today's date, send a message to info@transformedmindwellness.com, or notify the nearest Bible-believing church if you have taken this vital step toward salvation. Congratulations! I look forward to hearing from you.

HOW CAN I RECEIVE THE GIFT OF THE HOLY SPIRIT?

After the salvation step, you can ask for the gift of the Holy Spirit wherever you are or visit a Bible-believing Church. The Holy Spirit is the Spirit of adoption that bears witness with our spirit that we are the children of God. (Romans 8:14–17).

MENTAL HEALTH FAQS

IS FEELING SAD THE SAME AS DEPRESSION?

No, they differ in intensity and impact. Sadness is one of the natural human emotional reactions to a situation, and it's usually temporary. Depression is more significant in intensity, lasts longer, and can impair functioning.

HOW DO I KNOW IF I'M MENTALLY OR EMOTIONALLY UNWELL?

If your beliefs, thoughts, feelings, or behaviors persistently and significantly negatively impact your ability to function in a standard or ordinary way, it is crucial to seek professional help.

WHAT ARE THE RISK FACTORS OF SUICIDE?

Adverse Childhood Experiences, physical or mental health, access to firearms, past or current substance use problem, past suicide attempt or self-injurious behavior, loneliness, bullying, hopelessness, helplessness, impulsivity, mental health diagnosis, transgender, etc.

WHAT ARE THE PROTECTIVE FACTORS OF SUICIDE?

Future goals/orientation, coping strategies, reasons/purpose for living, support from family and friends, social connection, limited access to lethal means of suicide during emotional crisis, cultural/spiritual objections to suicide, parenthood, hopefulness, access to responsive crisis line, etc.

WHAT IS PROFESSIONAL HELP?

Professional help refers to any clinical or subclinical intervention or treatment provided by an individual with the approved licensure or credentialing to practice in this field.

WHAT WILL A PROFESSIONAL DO?

A professional will conduct a screening and evaluation using assessments such as the Patient Health Questionnaire (PHQ-9), Generalized Anxiety Disorder 7-item scale (GAD-7), and Mood Disorder Questionnaire (MDQ), among others.

A psychotherapist is a licensed mental health professional who intervenes in therapy using various modalities, including Cognitive Behavioral Therapy (CBT) and supportive therapy.

A psychiatrist is a physician who specializes in psychiatry and evaluates, diagnoses, and intervenes in therapy, either in combination with medication or through medication management specific to the underlying disorder, such as antidepressants, anxiolytics, mood stabilizers, and antipsychotics.

HOW CAN I GET PROFESSIONAL HELP?

There are peculiarities and differences with each state and country.

First, consider talking to a **trusted support,** such as a close friend, family member, pastor, mentor, etc., for low-level concerns. If symptoms don't improve or with an absence of trusted support, then you should consider the following:

Speak with your primary care provider to refer you to or collaborate with a psychotherapist or psychiatrist to alleviate the access gap for a mental health professional.

Contact your insurance provider to obtain a list of in-network providers, or search the internet for websites that offer a diverse range of providers and assess whether they are a potential fit based on their profiles.

Schedule an appointment to talk to a psychotherapist or a psychiatrist about your symptoms. Depending on the need, this may require one or a series of appointments.

If you don't have insurance, search the internet for free clinics, local mental health crisis lines, and the Department of Health and Human Services in your area.

Call your local crisis numbers (search the internet)

WHAT SHOULD YOU DO WHEN SOMEONE REACHES OUT TO YOU FOR HELP WITH AN EMOTIONAL OR MENTAL HEALTH ISSUE?

Ask and **listen** actively.

Provide **support** using the above resources.

Don't judge or criticize what you don't understand if you cannot be a safe and trusted place. Instead, encourage and refer to local mental health resources, including an emergency line, if thoughts of not wanting to be alive are present.

SPEAK UP! SEEK HELP! SUPPORT ANOTHER! SPREAD THE AWARENESS!

REFERENCES

Chapter One

1. Nagasako EM, Oaklander AL, Dworkin RH (February 2003). "Congenital Insensitivity to Pain: An Update." Pain. 101 (3):213–9. doi:10.1016/S0304-3959(02)00482-7. PMID 12583863. S2CID 206055264.

2. Shneidman, Edwin S. Suicide as psychache: A clinical approach to self-destructive behavior. Jason Aronson, 1993

Chapter Two

1. Tseng, J., Poppenk, J. Brain meta-state transitions demarcate thoughts across task contexts, exposing the mental noise of trait neuroticism. *Nat Commun* **11**, 3480 (2020). https://doi.org/10.1038/s41467-020-17255-9

REFERENCES

Chapter Three

1. Jacquelyn H. Flaskerud (2011) Heartbreak and Physical Pain Linked in Brain, Issues in Mental Health Nursing, 32:12, 789–791, DOI: 10.3109/01612840.2011.583714

2. Fast Facts: Preventing Child Sexual Abuse |Violence Prevention|Injury Center|CDC

3. "APA Dictionary of Psychology." American Psychological Association. Accessed July 13th, 2024. https://dictionary.apa.org/trauma.

4. Newman L. Elisabeth Kübler-Ross. BMJ. 2004;329(7466):627.

5. Stroebe, M, Schut H., & van den Bout, J. (2013). Complicated grief: Assessment of scientific knowledge and implications for research and practice. In M. Stroebe, H. Schut, & J. van den Bout (Eds.), Complicated grief: Scientific foundations for healthcare professionals (pp. 295–211). New York: Routledge.

6. Parkes CM. Bereavement in adult life. BMJ. 1998;316(7134):856–859. doi:10.1136/bmj.316.7134.856

Chapter Four

1. Caring for the Caregivers: The Critical Link Between Parent and Teen Mental Health—Making Caring Common (harvard.edu)

2. Steinbuchel PH, Wilens TE, Adamson JJ, Sgambati S. Posttraumatic stress disorder and substance use disorder in adolescent bipolar disorder. Bipolar Disord. 2009 Mar;11(2):198–204. doi: 10.1111/j.1399-5618.2008.00652x. PMID: 19267702; PMCID: PMC2917470.

3. Rice AS, Smith BH, Blyth FM. and Pain and the global burden of disease. Pain. 2016; 157: 791– 796.http://dx.doi.org/10.1097/j.pain.0000000000000454

Chapter Five

1. VanderWeele TJ, Li S, Tsai AC, Kawachi I. Association Between Religious Service Attendance and Lower Suicide Rates Among US Women. JAMA Psychiatry. 2016 Aug 1;73(8):845-51. doi:10.1001/jamapsychiatry.2016.1243. PMID: 27367927; PMCID: PMC7228478.

2. Poorolajal J, Goudarzi M, Gohari-Ensaf F, Darvishi N. Relationship of religion with suicidal ideation, suicide plan, suicide attempt, and suicide death: a meta-analysis. J Res Health Sci. 2022 Mar 2;22(1):e00537. doi:10.34172/jrhs.2022.72. PMID: 36511249; PMCID: PMC9315464.

3. Li S, Stampfer MJ, Williams DR, VanderWeele TJ. Association of Religious Service Attendance With Mortality Among Women. *JAMA Intern Med.* 2016;176(6):777–785. doi:10.1001/jamainternmed.2016.1615

4. D'Souza RF, Rodrigo A. Spiritually augmented cognitive behavioural therapy. Australas Psychiatry. 2004

Jun;12(2):148-52. doi: 10.1080/j.1039-8562.2004.02095.x. PMID: 15715760

Chapter Six

1. Bianconi, E., Piovesan, A., Facchin, F., Beraudi, A., Casadei, R., Frabetti, F., Vitale, L., Pelleri, M. C., Tassani, S., Piva, F., Perez-amodio, S., Strippoli, P. and Canaider, S. 2013. An estimator of the number of cells in a human body. Annals of Human Biology, 40 (6), pp 463–471

2. National Scientific Council on the Developing Child (2010). Early Experiences Can Alter Gene Expression and Affect Long-Term Development: Working Paper No. 10. Retrieved

3. "APA Dictionary of Psychology." American Psychological Association. Accessed July 27th, 2024. https://dictionary.apa.org/identity

4. DNA, Genes; Chromosomes Overview (clevelandclinic.org)

5. https://www.verywellmind.com/types-of-temperaments-7152818

6. Friedman, H., & Schustack, M. (2016). Personality: Classic Theories and Modern Research (Sixth ed.). Pearson Education

REFERENCES

Chapter Seven

1. https://doi.org/10.1016/j.jagp.2022.09.010

2. Khullar D. Finding Purpose for a Good Life. But Also a Healthy One. The New York Times. The Upshot. Jan. 1, 2018:1.

3. Musich S, Wang SS, Kraemer S, Hawkins K, Wicker E. Purpose in Life and Positive Health Outcomes Among Older Adults. Popul Health Manag. 2018 Apr;21(2):139-147. doi: 10.1089/pop.2017.0063. Epub 2017 Jul 5. PMID: 28677991; PMCID: PMC5906725.

4. Breitbart W, Rosenfeld B, Pessin H, Applebaum A, Kulikowski J, Lichtenthal WG. Meaning-centered group psychotherapy: an effective intervention for improving psychological well-being in patients with advanced cancer. J Clin Oncol. 2015 Mar 1;33(7):749–54. doi: 10.1200/JCO.2014.57.2198. Epub 2015 Feb 2. PMID: 25646186; PMCID: PMC4334778.

Chapter Eight

1. "Tongue-able interfaces: Prototyping and evaluating camera-based tongue gesture input system," Smart Health (2018)

2. IJIRT151445_PAPER.pdf

3. Michael A. Ferguson, Jared A. Nielsen, Jace B. King, Li Dai, Danielle M. Giangrasso, Rachel Holman, Julie

REFERENCES

R. Korenberg; Jeffrey S. Anderson (2018) Reward, salience, and attentional networks are activated by religious experience in devout Mormons, Social Neuroscience, 13:1, 104-116, DOI: 10.1080/17470919.2016.1257437

Chapter Nine

1. Bremner RH, Koole SL, Bushman BJ. "Pray for those who mistreat you": The Effects of Prayer on Anger and Aggression. Pers Soc Psychol Bull. 2011 Jun;37(6):830-7. doi: 10.1177/0146167211402215. Epub 2011 Mar 18. PMID: 21421766.

2. Boelens PA, Reeves RR, Replogle WH, Koenig HG. The effect of prayer on depression and anxiety: maintenance of positive influence one year after prayer intervention. Int J Psychiatry Med. 2012;43(1):85–98. doi: 10.2190/PM.43.1.f. PMID: 22641932.

3. Pargament KI, Koenig HG, Tarakeshwar N, Hahn J. Religious coping methods as predictors of psychological, physical and spiritual outcomes among medically ill elderly patients: a two-year longitudinal study. J Health Psychol. 2004 Nov;9(6):713–30. doi:10.1177/1359105304045366. PMID: 15367751.

Chapter Ten

1. Toussaint L, Gall AJ, Cheadle A, Williams DR. Editor's Choice: Let it rest: Sleep and health as positive correlates of forgiveness of others and self-forgiveness. Psychol Health. 2020 Mar;35(3):302-317. doi:

10.1080/08870446.2019.1644335. Epub 2019 Jul 31. PMID: 31364412; PMCID: PMC6992518.

Chapter Eleven

1. Emmons, R. A., & McCullough, M. E. (2003). Counting blessings versus burdens: An experimental investigation of gratitude and subjective well-being in daily life. Journal of Personality and Social Psychology, 84, 377-389. doi:10.1037/0022-3514.84.2.377

2. McCullough, M. E., Emmons, R. A., & Tsang, J. A. (2002). The Grateful Disposition: A Conceptual and Empirical Topography. Journal of Personality and Social Psychology, 82(1), 112–127.

3. Wood AM, Froh JJ, Geraghty AW. Gratitude and Well-being: A Review and Theoretical Integration. *Clin Psychol Rev*. 2010;30:890-905.

4. Landman, J. (1993). Regret: The persistence of the possible. Oxford University Press.

5. Bono, G., Emmons, R. A., & McCullough, M. E. (2004). Gratitude in Practice and the Practice of Gratitude. In P. A. S. Joseph (Ed.), Positive psychology in practice (pp. 464–481). John Wiley & Sons, Inc..

6. Cain IH, Cairo A, Duffy M, et al. Measuring gratitude at work. J Posit Psychol. 2018;14:440-451

7. O'Connell BH, O'Shea D, Gallagher S. Feeling Thanks and Saying Thanks: A Randomized Controlled Trial Examining If

REFERENCES

and How Socially Oriented Gratitude Journals Work. J Clin Psychol. 2017 Oct;73(10):1280-1300. doi: 10.1002/jclp.22469. Epub 2017 Mar 6. PMID: 28263399.

8. Lichtenstein-Vidne L, Okon-Singer H, Cohen N, et al. Attentional bias in clinical depression and anxiety: The impact of emotional and non-emotional distracting information. *Biol Psychol.* 2017;122:4-12. doi:10.1016/j.biopsycho.2016.07.012

Chapter Twelve

1. Setting the Stage: Neurobiological Effects of Music on the Brain by Samata R. Sharma and David Silbersweig (berklee.edu)

2. Beaty, R.E. (2015). The neuroscience of musical improvisation. Neuroscience & Biobehavioral Reviews, 51, 108–117.doi: 10.1016/j.neubiorev.2015.01.004

3. Kathleen A. Corrigall, Laurel J. Trainor; Associations Between Length of Music Training and Reading Skills in Children.Music Perception 1 December 2011; 29 (2): 147–155. doi: https://doi.org/10.1525/mp.2011.29.2.147

4. Pedersen W, Skrondal A. Ecstasy and new patterns of drug use: a normal population study.Addiction. 1999;94(11):1695-1706

5. Granot R, Spitz DH, Cherki BR, Loui P, Timmers R, Schaefer RS, Vuoskoski JK, Cárdenas-Soler RN,Soares-Quadros JF Jr,Li S, Lega C, La Rocca S, Martínez IC, Tanco M, Marchiano M,

REFERENCES

Martínez-Castilla P, Pérez-Acosta G, Martínez-Ezquerro JD, Gutiérrez-Blasco IM, Jiménez-Dabdoub L, Coers M, Treider JM, Greenberg DM, Israel S. Help! I Need Somebody& Music as a Global Resource for Obtaining Wellbeing Goals in Times of Crisis. Front Psychol. 2021 Apr 14;12:648013. doi:10.3389/fpsyg.2021.648013. PMID: 33935907; PMCID: PMC8079817.

6. Golden TL, Springs S, Kimmel HJ, Gupta S, Tiedemann A, Sandu CC, Magsamen S. The Use of Music in the Treatment and Management of Severe Mental Illness: A Global Scoping Review of the Literature. Front Psychol. 2021 Mar 31;12:649840. doi:10.3389/fpsyg.2021.649840. PMID: 33868127; PMCID: PMC8044514.

7. Matt Bradshaw, Christopher G. Ellison, Qijuan Fang, Collin Mueller, Listening to Religious Music and Mental Health in Later Life, The Gerontologist, Volume 55, Issue 6, December 2015, Pages 961–971, https://doi.org/10.1093/geront/gnu020.

8. Alexandra A. Johnson, Arron Berry, Maia Bradley, Jill A. Daniell, Claudia Lugo, Kristin Schaum-Comegys, Christine Villamero, Kelly Williams, Hohyung Yi, Elizabeth Scala, Madeleine Whalen. Examining the Effects of Music-Based Interventions on Pain and Anxiety in Hospitalized Children: An Integrative Review Journal of Pediatric Nursing, Volume 60,2021, Pages 71-76,

9. Reddick BH, Beresin EV. Rebellious Rhapsody: Metal, Rap, Community, and Individuation. Acad Psychiatry. 2002;26(1):51-59

REFERENCES

10. Trost W, Frühholz S, Schön D, Labbé C, Pichon S, Grandjean D, Vuilleumier P. Getting the beat: entrainment of brain activity by musical rhythm and pleasantness. Neuroimage. 2014 Dec;103:55–64. doi: 10.1016/j.neuroimage.2014.09.009. Epub 2014 Sep 16. PubMed PMID: 25224999.

11. Took KJ, Weiss DS. The relationship between heavy metal and rap music and adolescent turmoil: real or artifact? Adolescence. 1994;29(115):613–621

12. North AC, Hargreaves DJ. Problem music and self-harming. Suicide Life Threat Behav. 2006;36(5):582–590

13. Roberts KR, Dimsdale J, East P, Friedman L. Adolescent emotional response to music and its relationship to risk-taking behaviors. J Adolesc Health. 1998;23(1):49–54

14. Roberts DF, Christensen PG. Popular music in childhood and adolescence. In: Singer DG, Singer JL, eds. Handbook of Children and the Media. Thousand Oaks, CA: Sage Publications; 2001:395–410

15. Council on Communications and Media: The Impact of Music, Music Lyrics, and Music Videos on Children and Youth. Pediatrics. November 2009; 124(5): 1488–1494. 10.1542/peds.2009-2145

16. Fischer P, Greitemeyer T. Music, and aggression: the impact of sexual-aggressive song lyrics on aggression-related thoughts, emotions, and behavior toward the same and opposite sex. Pers Soc Psychol Bull. 2006;32(9):1165–1176

17. Rentfrow, P. J. (2012). The Role of Music in Everyday Life: Current Directions in the Social Psychology of Music. Social and Personality Psychology Compass, 6(5), 402–416. https://doi.org/10.1111/j.1751-9004.2012.00434.x

Chapter Fifteen

1. F.Barton Evana iii author of Harry Stack Sullivan: Interpersonal Theory and Psychotherapy (Makers of Modern Psychotherapy) 1st Edition

2. Stack-Sullivan Interpersonal Theory - Nursing Theory (nursing-theory.org)

3. Alexander F. Danvers, Liliane D. Efinger, Matthias R. Mehl, Peter J. Helm, Charles L. Raison, Angelina J. Polsinelli, Suzanne A. Moseley, David A. Sbarra, Loneliness and time alone in everyday life: A descriptive-exploratory study of subjective and objective social isolation, Journal of Research in Personality, Volume 107,2023,104426, ISSN 0092-6566.

4. Cassidy, J. (1994). Emotion regulation: Influences of attachment relationships.a Monographs of the Society for Research in Child Development, 59(2-3), 228–283.

5. Hazan, C. Shaver, P. (1987). Romantic love conceptualized as an attachment process. Journal of Personality and Social Psychology, 52(3), 511–5246.

6. Markus Kitayama, 1991; Shweder Bourne, 1984; Triandis, 1989)

ACKNOWLEDGMENTS

I extend my profound appreciation to God and the experiences of others for their inspiration in writing this book.

I'm deeply grateful to my husband, Obafemi, and children for their immense support, especially during the writing of this book. I also greatly appreciate the support of my parents, siblings, extended families, teachers, mentors, mentees, colleagues, and friends.

My sincere gratitude to Mrs. Olajumoke Adenowo for her mentorship and guidance.

Several individuals deserve recognition for their invaluable support, including those who provided unofficial beta reading for this book. I'm thankful for Dr. Ekundayo and Donna Partow's writing resources.

My sincerest thanks to Abisola Orimoloye for her expertise in editing this book.

And special thanks to you for investing in yourself and your loved ones.

ABOUT THE AUTHOR

Dr. Tiwalola Osunfisan, also known as Dr. Tiwa, is a double-board-certified psychiatrist

specializing in general psychiatry and consultation-liaison psychiatry. A behavioral health integration expert, assistant professor, global speaker, mental health ambassador, and mindset strategist, Dr. Tiwa is also a John Maxwell-certified speaker, facilitator, and coach. With a passion for increasing mental health awareness, Dr. Tiwa integrates mind, body, and faith to promote mental wellness and transformation.

In addition to practicing psychiatry, Dr. Tiwa is the founder of Transformed Mind Wellness, LLC, a virtual company offering mental health-related speaking engagements, training, and faith-based coaching services. These services are designed to help healthcare professionals and highly skilled individuals achieve sustained mental performance and transformation in every area of life.

Believing that emotional intelligence, mastery, and purposeful living are crucial for growth and fulfillment, Dr. Tiwa equips individuals to face life's challenges with courage, clarity, resilience, and intention. Featured in publications, speaking engagements, and podcasts on various mental health topics, Dr. Tiwa is a dedicated mentor and teacher, committed to sharing knowledge and making a positive impact on others.

Dr. Tiwa is married to Obafemi, and they have three children. They reside in the United States.

A NOTE TO YOU, THE READER:

Thank you for reading this book. As part of writing this book, I hope to connect with you and encourage you to heal and transform your life. I hope I've provided you with some motivation and tools for growth and maturity to help you handle the past or day-to-day challenges that you may have faced.

COULD YOU PLEASE DO ME A FAVOR?

I put my heart and soul into writing this book, spending hundreds of hours and many days and nights on it. It's been a massive project that I've taken about 2.5 years to complete. This book means a lot to me. It's my way of motivating and inspiring you, your generation, and other readers to heal and be great. Can you take a moment to leave your heartfelt comments on Amazon? Your review will help someone who hasn't read the book yet know what you liked about it and why they should take their time to read it.

A NOTE TO YOU, THE READER:

I appreciate receiving honest feedback and will read every review from you. Reviews make a HUGE difference to an author. Writing a review is the very best way to help me out :)

To post your review for *When the Mind Cries*, please visit: https://transformedmindwellness.com/offerings/#book

For online courses on various topics, including "purposeful living," "from self-doubt to bold action," and many more, please visit https://transformedmindwellness.com/offerings/

You can connect with me via:
www.transformedmindwellness.com
On Instagram and YouTube: @talktodrtiwa

For inquiries regarding collaborations, speaking, training, and coaching, send an email to:
info@transformedmindwellness.com
or visit www.transformedmindwellness.com

www.ingramcontent.com/pod-product-compliance
Lightning Source LLC
Chambersburg PA
CBHW060451030426
42337CB00015B/1552